Praise for
Unbox Your Relationships

"Tobias Beck's book, *Unbox Your Relationships: How to Attract the Right People and Build Relationships that Last*, is the perfect antidote for people looking to improve relationships—with themselves and others. In this book, Tobias shows you how to take control of your destiny by successfully managing your closest relationships. Insightful, funny at times, and creative, this book is a must-read for anyone who wants to live their best life by connecting with the world around them."

—**Scott Miller**, *Wall Street Journal* bestselling author and former Chief Marketing Officer, FranklinCovey Co.

"Tobias Beck has written a book that will have you thinking about relationships outside of the box. *Unbox Your Relationships: How to Attract the Right People and Build Relationships that Last* is essential for those looking to feel more connected with the world around them. Beck not only shows you how to make the most out of your personal relationships, he also shows you exactly what kind of person you are and why you matter. Read this book if you are looking to improve how you relate and connect to your friends, your partner, your colleague—and yourself."

—**MJ Fievre**, author of the poetry collection *Happy, Okay?* and the bestselling Badass Black Girl book series

Praise for Tobias Beck

"Unbox Your Life will help you do just that—unbox your life and in the process discover your life's mission. Personal discovery and sense of self-worth is the foundation of any healthy relationship which is why the private victory must precede the public victory. This book is a must-read for anyone looking to build relationships that last."

—**Sean Covey**, President, FranklinCovey Education and *New York Times* bestselling coauthor of *The 4 Disciplines of Execution*

"Tobias shares his struggles and triumphs with raw honesty. This book is a gem. It will help you form amazing relationships, not only with others, but also with yourself."

—**John Strelecky**, author of *The Why Café* and *The Big Five for Life*

"Tobias Beck is a remarkable coach."

—**Daniel Aminati**, entertainer and TV Host (*Pro7*)

UN
BOX

YOUR RELATIONSHIPS!

UN
BOX

YOUR RELATIONSHIPS!

How to Attract
the Right People
and Build
Relationships
That Last

By Tobias Beck

mango
PUBLISHING GROUP
CORAL GABLES

Cover Design: total italic (Thierry Wijnberg), Amsterdam/Berlin
Cover Photo: © Karepa / © Vitalina Rybakova | Fotolia
Illustrations: Marvin Clifford
Interior Design: Lohse Design, Heppenheim | www.lohse-design.de
Production Design (English): Katia Mena
Author Photo: Patrick Reymann

For permission requests, please contact the publisher at:
Mango Publishing Group
2850 S Douglas Road, 4th Floor
Coral Gables, FL 33134 USA
info@mango.bz

For special orders, quantity sales, course adoptions and corporate sales, please email the publisher at sales@mango.bz. For trade and wholesale sales, please contact Ingram Publisher Services at customer.service@ingramcontent.com or + 1.800.509.4887.

Unbox Your Relationships: How to Attract the Right People and Build Relationships That Last

Library of Congress Cataloging-in-Publication number: 2021938177
ISBN: (print) 978-1-64250-650-1, (ebook) 978-1-64250-651-8
BISAC category code SEL040000, SELF-HELP / Communication & Social Skills

Printed in the United States of America

Table of Contents

Prologue

Have I loved?
Have I helped others to love?
Have I raised others up?
Have I left footprints on others' hearts instead of leaving them empty?

Older people sometimes ask curious questions that I, as a community service worker at the tender age of eighteen, did not understand much about.

Who were these "others," and was life not about making the most of my own journey? No, I came to learn; this was not the case. Life is about so much more. We, as individuals, are not the cornerstone of our existence.

> If there's one thing that's now become clear, it's that our relationships with others are our only constants in life—whether we want them or not.

Since the beginning of time, we have been programmed to connect with other people. But in a world where any and every wish can be satisfied with the swipe of a smartphone, it's easy to forget this. Next time you make a decision that deliberately leaves your options open, I invite you instead to take responsibility—for someone, something, anything. People are not products to be consumed and then left empty. Our hearts can handle plenty, but they cannot simply be regenerated at will.

Start by choosing a film on Netflix and watching it through to the end instead of checking the reviews to see if there's anything better.

Ride it out; breathe; feel it. Give things a chance instead of drawing rash conclusions.

We live in an age in which thousands of young people are permanently preoccupied with the quest for self-realization. But this is, for all intents and purposes, a relatively new thing: at no other time in history have we had the opportunity to shape our lives according to our own visions and values, and it has never been available to more than a small, privileged section of the population. Moreover, in this desperate striving to be all that we wish to be, we too often forget the foundation of our existence: family. Family means so much more than similar genetics—they're the people with whom we feel at home and by whom we are loved unconditionally, simply for being who we are.

Perhaps the people I'm describing are no longer or have never been in your life. If this is the case, please don't set this book to one side. Understand that even if you feel alone, you never are. The people you are looking for are also looking for you; you simply need to open your heart and let others into your life again.

We live in a world that strives for perfection and forgets that relationships are not a filtered Instagram snapshot. Relationships exist alongside and because of us and, as such, are also like us: unique, flawed, and constantly changing. This is a good thing. Perfection is far too static a state for the colorful emotional world in which our relationships reside. We need relationships to be happy, yet it is this dynamic emotional world that makes it so difficult for us to establish them in the first place.

In the first part of this book, I'll take you on a journey of discovery to yourself and the people in your life. We'll explore together how you can achieve fulfilled relationships with yourself and others, despite each one of them being as unique and individual as you are.

In the second part of the book, I'll introduce my animal-based model of the four basic types of humans: whale, shark, dolphin, and owl. This model has already inspired millions online, saved marriages, turned offices into creative spaces, resolved disputes, and engendered understanding. You should be looking forward to getting to know the animal inside of you because rest assured, one exists. There might even be more than one at the same time! Once you've discovered your animal, you'll also find out how it's linked to a certain millennia-old mystery.

As you read, I wish you plenty of enjoyment, memorable moments with yourself and "others," and a productive journey of discovery.

When Freedom Makes Us Lonely

Thanks to our networked world, we have more relationships than ever before. We've never been in touch with so many people at any one time, and it's never been so hard for us to open up to one another. But this hasn't always been the case.

We were conceived because of our parents' relationship with one another, and recent studies have shown that an infant who is nourished solely by food will not survive long. We need social relationships and emotional ties to exist and thrive. What's more, we require them at a certain level of intensity to lead a happy and fulfilling life because the quality of our relationships—private and professional—is what determines our overall satisfaction.

Nothing about this state of affairs has changed in the last millennia. What has changed is the world in which we are required to form these relationships. Just a few decades ago, it was usual—even vital for survival—that a person never left their village, their immediate environment, and the people they grew up with. They might marry and move into the neighboring village, but there, too, were rigid social structures to be integrated into several generations often living together under one roof.

In this network of relationships based on small villages and settlements, everyone had a place and a defined role. People knew and trusted each other. Business dealings were based on verbal contracts, and depending on the region in which people grew up, religion was of great importance. The belief in something greater was a common source of solace in bad times. This form of coexistence provided protection, security, and a sense of affinity for the community. But the

Unbox Your Relationships

possibilities for realizing oneself as an individual were limited, and the collective character of coexistence restricted individual freedom. The daughter of the baker always became a baker herself and would never dream of opening her own clothing store or designing high heels in neon colors.

When times changed, they did so rapidly. For us as humans, the evolution from collective community to anonymous individuals progressed so quickly that we sometimes struggle to keep up: we chase our lives breathlessly in an attempt not to let them get completely out of sight. In the anonymity of the twenty-first century, we suddenly have more freedom than is good for us. Our fear of missing out is so great that endless choice renders us unable to decide.

As soon as we have decided on one thing, another automatically becomes more appealing. We move restlessly from one city to another, across continents: here today, there tomorrow. Wherever we are, we find new people whose language we speak purely because we're in the same boat. We feel lonely together, no longer daring to open up to one another or to choose people who might not choose us. We fear rejection. We fear that people will leave us tomorrow for newer and better adventures. We have become globetrotters without roots or responsibilities. The security, comfort, and sense of belonging we used to get from a whole village we now seek from a single person: our partner.

The happiness of a family hinges more than ever on the relationship of the partners. But because we are unable to be all things to one person at the same time, and because we have forgotten how to fulfill our needs from many different relationships, we have more single households than families—especially in urban areas. Worldwide, almost every third marriage now ends in divorce, and more children are growing up with separated parents than ever before.

For the first time in human history, it is possible for humans to define the meaning and direction of their own lives, and many of us are privileged enough to be among this number. If we want to become a deep-sea diver in the Caribbean and crack open a fresh coconut in the evenings under a palm-leaf roof, we live in a world where this is a possibility. By the same token, if we want to become a cardiac surgeon, buy an apartment on the Upper East Side, and change the human world forever with our work, this is a reachable goal for many of us.

The problem is that we, as humans, were not designed to have this level of freedom. Our modern life expectancy is four times the average lifespan of humans that lived during the Middle Ages, and many people reach or exceed it. We "break camp," reinvent ourselves, start from scratch because we have the freedom to do so. We have the freedom to change our minds or to commit to nothing—which we often do because the many available options make us dizzy with choice.

We are scared to choose an option that makes all others impossible; in fact, the freedom to be able to do anything is what also threatens to make us lonely. This is because what we need to live a happy and fulfilling life is a reliable network of committed relationships with people we love. We need people who—despite all the freedom on offer, the myriad choices open to us, and all our opportunities for self-realization—provide us comfort, reflect our values, and give us the security of being loved.

To avoid losing ourselves in a world of possibilities, it is vital that we remember our need for relationships and regain the ability to relate to one another. That's why in the first part of this book, I invite you to come on a journey with me to the best relationships of your life.

You've Always Been Enough

Have you ever thought about who you talk to most during the day? Without having ever met you, I know who this person is, and I also know you're not shy to say what you think to them. This talk is the straightest of straight talk, and your feedback is free from glitter and rainbows. You put all nonsense aside, leave out the niceties, and concentrate on what really matters: where you are falling short and how you could be better.

It begins in the morning, before the first coffee when you stumble over the scale on your way to the shower and launch into the first tirade. "Why do you keep gaining weight? You could really have done without the milk chocolate and the luxury chips in bed last night in front of the TV." Perhaps you stand in front of the mirror in the morning and comment blithely on your thinning hair, your wrinkles—and, for good measure, your bulbous nose, crooked toes, the state of your messy apartment, your non-existent fitness levels, or, depending on how you're feeling that day, the very existence of your imperfect, undisciplined life.

I'm sure you wouldn't allow a single person around you to talk about you as you sometimes do about yourself.

> There's one person you talk to without pause your whole life long: yourself!

On average, you think 60,000 thoughts a day. If you take a moment to be completely honest with yourself, you'll find you often phrase these thoughts in a tone for which you'd instantly cut off partners or friends—without explanation and with no chance for forgiveness.

You wouldn't tolerate it for a second, and yet you allow your inner voice to follow you around, make you feel guilty, and brand you as the hopeless cluster of cells you think you are. Tell me: *how can this make any sense?*

Aside from the fact that these statements bear little or no relation to reality, there's one other reason they're especially harmful. If we say things often enough, we start to believe them.

Read this sentence again because it's crucial:

> If we say things to ourselves enough, we start to believe them!

What happens if we hold fast to a particular belief in something, even though it's not the case? At some point, our brains cannot tell if the things we incessantly tell ourselves are true or fiction. They cannot tell if the invisible voice that chases us around and disapprovingly refers to every chocolate bar as a "failure" is correct or talking absolute nonsense. Once they have heard it enough times, our brains simply start to believe it.

Later in the cycle, the things we believe are manifested in our lives. Our beliefs about ourselves are made tangible in countless ways: our demeanor, our body language, our voice, our salary negotiations, our next date, our presentations, our children's education, our friendships, and all our relationships with others. Our inner voice influences our whole life, and although other people cannot hear it, they can sense it in the way we relate to ourselves.

At this juncture, let me offer some advice: The only thing your inner voice should be telling you each morning—in front of the bathroom mirror, pre-shower, with scruffy pajamas and bad breath—is that you are the greatest, most beautiful, and brightest star under the sun. Anything else? It's talking nonsense. Has that made you chuckle?

Chuckle away—laughing breaks down stress hormones. But don't forget the real message: that you *are* great. Your talents, big and small, are valuable. Take a moment to reflect on all you have achieved. Write down what you have to be proud of. If the space here is not enough, get a flipchart and fill it up in size six font.

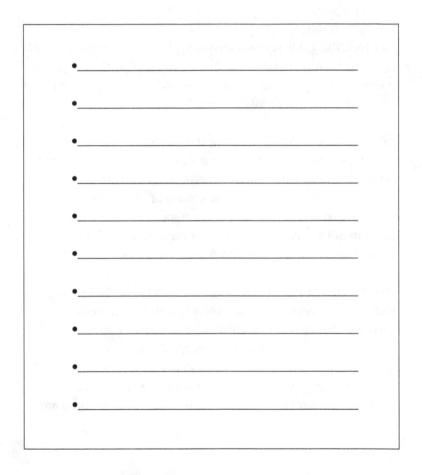

I know that at some point in your life—maybe even a few times too many—you have stood breathless and exhausted at a crossroads, then sat down and cried bitterly on the cold, hard asphalt. You didn't know what to do anymore. You felt alone, with no idea how to take the next step, let alone how to decide on the direction. But I also know that you summoned all your courage and your last ounce of energy and just went on.

Before you read on, can you give yourself a hug for each time you stood up again?

"But Tobi, I've made so many mistakes." Really? Me too—and that's a good thing. Mistakes make us human and give us the opportunity to keep learning. I make mistakes time and again, but I learn from them and make better mistakes next time.

Only when you start to be forgiving of yourself, to be kind to yourself in the face of setbacks, and to show yourself the same appreciation as you do others can you really begin to love yourself. Once this happens, you'll no longer need two slabs of chocolate and a main course of luxury chips to dim the frustration. You'll no longer need the cigarettes you cling to feverishly or the gallons of alcohol you use to forget about what you are but do not want to be.

Once you start to love yourself, you'll no longer need all the things the world says you need to be better, more beautiful, or more desirable. If you think about it, the flip side of these advertising messages is that without these things, you are not enough. You need the makeup that makes you "flawless," the statement watch that earns you clout, the sports car to impress your date, or the hundredth anti-cellulite gel for ninety-nine pounds a pot. But the truth is, you don't need any of it, because:

You've always been enough.

You've always been adorable, unique, and desirable, just as you are. However, you rarely hear this message in the modern world—if you acknowledged it, you'd stop consuming all the things listed above.

How do we reprogram our inner voice? To do so, we must begin listening to ourselves carefully and often, constantly asking ourselves what kind of untruths it might be telling. The most dangerous thing about this habit is when we fail to realize we are even doing it. The familiar becomes automatic and, at some point, occurs on a completely unconscious basis. Much of what we tell ourselves consists of old beliefs that we picked up in childhood or adolescence. Children—as we must constantly bear in mind when we become parents ourselves—suck up everything they hear like a sponge and believe it, some of it for the rest of their lives.

Deep down inside you is a little version of yourself that never gets older. If you're willing to embrace it, we'll go on a journey with this little "you" in the next chapter.

This little "you" stays four years old forever and believes every sentence you say. Everything you say to them is their reality, and thus also yours. No matter how old you are, your inner voice speaks to the little boy or girl inside you, and they flinch every time they hear that they are not valuable, pretty, successful, ambitious, thin, or disciplined enough—that they are not enough, were not enough, and will never be enough.

What no one ever tells us is that once we become adults, it is our job to take care of ourselves. We hold firm to the belief that others will always be there to do it for us. Because our parents took care of us for so long, we go out into life and search for a replacement: a new "parent" in the form of a partner.

Many of us become reliant on the care of others. We let others determine how we feel and forget that we can control it ourselves. It is not another's love for us that begins a happy relationship, but rather, our love for ourselves.

A Journey to Your Inner Child

Want to improve your relationship? Congratulations: this is an admirable goal. To achieve it, however, there's one key point you'll need to address, and whether you treat it as a stumbling block or an amazing opportunity is up to you. Before you can establish a truly resilient bond with another, there's one person with whom you'll need to make peace and fall in love all over again: yourself.

Perhaps this sentence caused you to pause for a breath. That's okay. Take time to inhale and exhale slowly, then read through the following exercise and join me on a journey to the person deep inside you. There is a young boy or girl who has yearned, for years, to connect with you. Perhaps your access to this inner child has been muddied— buried by self-doubt, disparaging statements (spoken by others, then assimilated into your own self-talk), pain, and negative experiences. Now, I invite you to let go. The things you'll learn when you reopen these channels will change your life and your relationships forever.

Play the piece of music above, or simply enjoy the silence. No matter how you focus best, you should remain undisturbed for at least ten minutes.

Sit on a chair, comfortable but upright. Roll your shoulders up and back to loosen your spine, place both feet on the floor, and close your eyes.

You may start to notice small sounds around you; you might hear your breathing and perceive the thoughts that race through your head. Let them go; do not assign them any significance. You may start to be aware of your body, your pelvic bones and legs, your stomach, shoulders, arms, and head. Breathe.

You might feel your heart beating; with every heartbeat, you relax a little more. Allow the rhythmic beating to draw you ever further into your inner world. Imagine you have light weights hanging from your hands and feet, and with every breath, they become a little heavier. You become ever more deeply immersed in a state of calm and relaxation. Let your breath and heartbeat carry you inside yourself.

If spontaneous thoughts persist, know that this is completely natural. Let them waft like clouds over your consciousness; concentrate on your breathing and heartbeat. This time is for you and you alone.

As you immerse yourself deeper in this state of relaxation, imagine yourself leaving your body and floating in the air. Picture yourself leaving the room you are sitting in and floating into another one somewhere in your consciousness.

As you breathe, each breath delivers you deeper into a state of reassuring warmth.

You land in this other room, feel the floor under your feet, and look around. On each wall, you see pictures hanging—pictures upon pictures. As you look more closely, you see that all of them are photographs; not only that, they are photographs of you. You see yourself in every corner and can scarcely believe your eyes. The images show you on your journey through life: from where you are now back to your first seconds outside the womb.

You move through the room as if moving along a timeline, becoming younger with every image. You are twenty, then eighteen; you see yourself driving a car for the first time or at your first workplace. You see yourself as a teenager, laughing with friends, then as a ten-year-old child on the way to school. With every photograph, you travel further back in your life. Finally, you see yourself as a small child: five, four, then three years old. Your smile is radiant, and you dance, jump, and laugh with joy.

As you move, astonished, through this inner chamber of consciousness, you feel a brush against your right hand. Someone is reaching gently for your fingers, pushing their little hand into yours. Amazed, you look down and see a small child in front of you. Your eyes meet, and you realize: there you are, at the age of just two or three.

You feel a further wave of astonishment and joy rising deep within you, surging through your body as you look into each other's eyes. "Wow," you realize, "that's me!"

The child looks you in the eye and begins to sob. As the tears stream down their face, they speak aloud. "Finally!" they say. "Finally, you're here! I've waited for you for so long!"

If at this point, you feel intense emotions attempting to surface, let them. Give them space, allow them free rein.

"I've missed you so much!" the child cries. "Every day, you put on a mask and hide yourself! Please, please, play with me again!"

You look the child deep in the eyes, follow your intuition and your heart, stretch out your hand, and take the child in your arms—loving, strong, full of joy. You envelop them in your embrace, hold them close to your heart, and connect with them. The bond between your hearts grows tighter; you feel the energy and deep love between you finally allowed to flow once again.

The child quivers in your arms, full at once of deep emotion, tears, laughter, and joy. That you are there is the only thing they wish for. They long for you not to be locked in a performance of adulthood, to remember to play, laugh, and snuggle with them, to devote yourself to them. They want to be close to you.

As you bury your face in the child's soft hair, you feel a surge of incomparable, unconditional love, deep and unending. In your mind, you speak to the child. "I love you," you say. "I care about you. I love you because you are the only thing I really have in this world. I promise to take care of you because if I love you, I can love others too!"

In your thoughts, you hug the little one tightly and feel your two hearts beating together. You take each other in; your gazes meet once more; you see the face of the child in front of you. Before it's time for you both to leave, you bestow the child with a beautiful, powerful gift for their journey. You bid them goodbye with love—in word and in feeling.

Suddenly, you notice that the room around you beginning to spin—first slowly, then increasingly quickly. You and the child spin with it, the child in your arms, as safe and full of lightness as on a summer's day on the beach. Their face beams with happiness. Suddenly, amidst this profound moment of joy, a realization descends. This is reality! This child is always with you—this lightness, joy, and deep love are always there. What's more, this is something no one can ever take away.

You spin for few more seconds, then gradually prepare to return to the room where your journey began. You take a deep breath, then count down slowly from five.

Five

You leave the beach and channel your consciousness to return to your body.

Four

You begin to feel your legs and arms. You feel yourself sitting in your chair and perceive the room around you.

Three

You imagine fresh, crystal-clear spring water lapping about your head and your consciousness, energizing you and waking you up.

Two

You take a deep breath and feel free and full of love.

One

You're back in the here and now.

Affirmations for Your Dialogue with Your Inner Child

"It's amazing that you're here, and it's amazing that you are exactly how you are."

"You are perfect. It's only a shame that the people around you have so often failed to notice it."

"Thank you for everything you have endured. You are so strong."

"Before, I wasn't able to appreciate you, but I promise never to let you be overburdened or ignored again."

"I'll never leave you to the mercy of strangers again. For me, you are number one."

"Leave the difficult stuff to me in the future; your job is to be a child. You can play, laugh, or even be sad if you want to. Never fear—I'll be keeping watch."

A Parent's Love

"It is a strange thing, but parents are people too; and when it comes to producing and raising offspring, they are no more adept than unskilled workers."

—VICCO VON BÜLOW (LORIOT)

There's a Japanese proverb that says: "It is only once one has children that one recognizes the greatness of a parent's love." Since becoming a father, I can attest to its veracity. There is much we can only understand once we have children ourselves: the love for a small person that *we* helped create, the worry about whether they have all they need, and above all, the worry that we as parents could fail at our immense task.

As a father to my children Maya and Emil, I am something of a tour guide on life's journey of adventure. My task, as I see it, is to build their strengths and recognize that as tiny humans, they consist of a body, a mind, and a soul. I believe that each of us, as humans, has our very own "soul plan"—if we allow ourselves to follow it, we will flourish. As such, it's important to me that my children understand they are loved unconditionally, that they are enough and perfect, just as they are. All babies are born without prejudice. I do not wish to impose my view of the world on them but to share special moments with them, help them lay deep roots, and encourage them to find their paths without taking away any of their agency in the process.

My wife Rita and I do not wish for our children to be carbon copies of ourselves or that they pursue our own missed opportunities and ambitions. That can never be sustainable because, ultimately, it only serves the parents' wishes.

Over the years, I've witnessed some great ways of letting children explore their passions independently. The one that stands out most, however, is a special children's orchestra: one that remained in my mind long after I'd heard it.

As part of this orchestra, children are let loose once a year in the instrument storage room, where they're permitted to pick out an instrument purely of their own choosing. Thus, it can happen, for example, that a gentle six-year-old girl points to a huge tuba and proudly drags it onto the stage.

Once all children have made their decisions, they stand behind a thick curtain. Then, the magic occurs: the curtain is lifted on a jam-packed concert hall, and the audience stands and applauds with vigor. The children aren't even required to play; instead, they are allowed to simply "be." Amazingly, in most cases, they go on to practice their chosen instrument independently, so enchanted by the atmosphere in which that first encounter took place.

As we've already learned, all humans, whether adults or children, have an innate longing for love. In the ideal case, this love goes through several stages:

1. As babies, we demand love with vigorous crying and are often comforted and cuddled in our parents' arms.
2. Sometime later, we learn that we receive love when we do something to earn it or when we give love ourselves.
3. We love without convention and without expecting anything in return. By this stage, we are rich in love.
4. The highest level is the ability to love even when we've been hurt.

Sadly, even in adulthood, some people resort to crying for love and attention. Clearly, they have not succeeded in progressing through the stages. But why? Why do some people linger at an undeveloped level while others learn to love despite hurt? Why do some develop an unwavering level of basic trust while others search their whole lives and never find it in themselves or in others? Why are some people able to build stable relationships apparently without thinking about it while others are disappointed again and again?

In childhood, it is the role of our parents not only to explain the world to us but to demonstrate it in all its rich shades. They show us what love is and how to live it. They teach us what we need to do to be loved or, in the best-case scenario, that being loved isn't a transaction. They determine the boundaries of what is good and what is bad. As children, we absorb all of this like sponges because, at that point, we don't know any better. Above all, we trust. We trust intuitively while adults struggle to trust at all or require a generous safety net. Children are born with an innate level of trust in the fact that no one means badly toward them and that, above all, their parents want the best for them.

Incidentally, I believe this also applies in cases where parents and grown-up children no longer communicate regularly. Simply: parents always want the best for their children, whereby this "best" is defined by the parents' value systems. This, in turn, is absorbed largely from *their* parents, and it is not uncommon for these values to be passed down wholesale from one generation to the next.

This is likely how you obtained some of the beliefs that are incongruous with your current reality—and which, as a result, you can reasonably strike from your worldview. "Nothing in life comes for free" is an obvious example. Certainly, in the harsh years that followed World War II, such a warning was justified; it existed for a reason and was more or less correct. Admittedly, love was free back then as it is today, but humans can't subsist on love alone. Nowadays, we live in a prosperous and benevolent society—one in which many people have all they need and are keen to give back when they can.

This means we get several things for "free," without an ulterior motive or the expectation of anything in return.

These things don't necessarily need to be material in nature—often, it's the case that those who have fortified their mental, spiritual, or intellectual reserves are willing to help others do the same. Of course, on the other hand, there are a few places where "nothing comes for free" is still an everyday reality. There are places where people struggle even to maintain their own reserves, and this is sad enough in itself.

Perhaps your parents often told you that you were a "worry wart," and so, as an adult, you shy away from new challenges. Perhaps you were always a "failure" at math because you only came home with Cs and Ds. Likely, this will have shaken your confidence such that your aversion to the subject persists today: as soon as you're required to add up in your head, your brain turns to mush, and three times three makes six. You and I know that this is *not* due to a fundamental lack of mathematical ability.

Perhaps you've spent years engaging with a different doctrine for life; perhaps you forged a career because of pressure from your mother. "My daughter will do things differently than me," she might have said. "My daughter won't have children so early; my daughter will complete her studies." Perhaps, in secret, you felt lonely because you wanted something else: a family, a house in the countryside, a comfortable middle-class existence. But even without knowing it, you lived out your mother's projections—the life that you willingly learned.

Wherever and however these beliefs originated, I'm quite certain that it was never your parents' intention to make things hard for you. On the contrary—your parents love you and want the best for you. Might they have sometimes been impatient in the way they conveyed this? Of course. Might there have been phases in which they prioritized their needs over your own? Probably. Did they replicate patterns they'd picked up from their parents and perpetuate them with little reflection? Almost definitely. Why? Because parents are people too, and because children are the most wonderful but often also the most tiring and challenging gift one could wish for. As parents, we must find our own balance between two ultimately incompatible things: the desire to keep our children close and, at the same time, allowing them to spread their wings. This is one of the greatest challenges of all, and as such, it's quite normal to occasionally give more weight to one desire than the other.

Even if it seems a rather fanciful notion, I like to think that we choose our parents. After a long search, I settled on Erika and Horst Beck from Wuppertal: the only people in the universe willing to take on and lovingly mentor a chaotic non-conformist like me. Looking back, I am particularly thankful for the primal trust they placed in me. I knew that I could always come back home and be loved unconditionally, without having to do anything in return. My parents always made me feel that I was "enough" and that, one day, I'd make something great of myself.

When it came to what this "something" was, they were relatively unspecific; in fact, they displayed incredible patience with my ever-changing whims. Even as my peers began to formulate solid future plans, my "plan" shifted on a weekly basis. From doctor to zoologist to importer of Alaskan blueberries, nothing was off the table—and with each new idea, my parents worked steadfastly to ensure that I felt supported and valid. Their support always brought me happiness. My parents deserve a heartfelt thanks for allowing me to spread my wings and, in turn, help others fly and be the best versions of themselves. My parents didn't always have it easy with me, and it's only thanks to their example that I can guide my own children in the way they deserve.

"Children who are loved grow into loving adults."

From the start of their lives, children are tiny, fully formed personalities, each equipped with their own character traits and an irrepressible will. They come into the world with their own sense of "why." Sometimes, they are so similar to us that it is difficult to distinguish their wishes and desires from our own; sometimes, their sense of "why" is so foreign to us that we must look far behind our own horizons to understand it. Some parents succeed in doing this; others are rather more poorly equipped. This is not because they are ill-intentioned (and let me be clear, this book is not intended to touch on abuse or neglect of any kind), but rather because, in some cases, their sense of "why" has so long been buried. Other times, they may simply lack the energy or the capacity for self-reflection; in the worst-case scenario, all these factors may converge at once.

The older we become, the more difficult we find it to process the changes around us and to integrate them into our world. We're all familiar with the saying, "Everything was better as it used to be." While this doesn't apply as a universal truth, it *is* true that at some point, our internal "hard discs" become full and our experiences so entrenched that our brains find it difficult to form new connections. At their relatively older age, some parents find this easier than others.

And even when parents realize that they have got something—or many things—wrong, they often find it hard to admit. Perhaps they weren't there for their child when they needed them and worry they wouldn't be able to live with the admission. Sometimes, we need to accept an apology we know we're never going to receive—not for our parents' sake but for our own. Our parents did the best they could, and whatever we lacked in our childhood and youth is a piece of the puzzle that's now gone for good. We must rid ourselves of the notion that, at some point, we can recover it. All we can do is fill the gap of our own accord by striving to forgive.

At some point, it comes time to break away from the people who raised us, to remember the good memories and forgive them for the bad such that we can let them go in love and peace. Moreover, our parents no longer necessarily need to be alive for us to do this. The beauty of forgiveness is that you only need yourself to carry it out.

Which beliefs about yourself and the world have you absorbed unconsciously from your parents? Think about them and write them down. If you judge certain beliefs to be correct and beneficial and thus wish to retain them, great. If, on the other hand, you find a belief difficult to support or justify, cross it out and practice consciously removing it from your thoughts the next time it occurs to you.

- _____
- _____
- _____
- _____
- _____
- _____
- _____
- _____
- _____
- _____

The Trip of Your Life

How often do you look over the shoulder of a colleague at work and think, *Well, you can do it that way, but it isn't effective?* And how often, when you see the result, do you have to ungrudgingly concede, *Actually, that wasn't so stupid after all?*

Many people are different than you.

Not just different, but *fundamentally* different. They reason things in ways you would never dream of, solve problems in their own manner, and dream of different adventures than you. That's a good thing; that's what makes our world colorful and exciting. Some people need to jump out of a helicopter with skis to feel alive, while for others, slicing bread by hand is life on the edge. The fact that it is difficult to find common ground with some people does not make things impossible.

Not all characters at Disneyland are the same, but at the end of the day, everybody is celebrating together, with glitter, confetti, and a huge dose of fun. And that's what it's about. We only have this one trip; our time is limited.

If all of us had just one vacation, the chance to take one big journey in our lives, would we spend it comparing ourselves with others, or would we listen excitedly to those we met, learning about how they think and wishing them a wonderful time?

> The journey in the paragraph above really exists.
> It's your life!

What differentiates the adventurers of the world from the package tourists is that the latter spend their travels firmly in their comfort zone. They want nothing more than to surround themselves with similar people and spend the day whining about others—those who happen to have better weather, to pay less, or to pick the shorter line. But it makes little sense to waste days in this way.

On the other hand, adventurers know that on their journey, they should listen to the experiences of fellow travelers, learn from them, and recognize that an adventure shared is the best kind of fun.

In my eyes, the journey of life is a bit like taking a coach trip—not a fully air-conditioned five-star model, but the kind that gets a puncture in the middle of the South American plains. The kind whose air conditioning fails at thirty degrees in the shade and whose toilet is clogged at precisely the moment you get an upset stomach. This is travelling outside your comfort zone, with all the stops, detours, and calamities that adventurers experience on their one, grand life journey.

In life, we board our bus, meet our parents, and initially believe they'll always travel with us. Though we eventually learn that this is not the case, many more travelers will board to take their place: siblings, cousins, mentors, and friends. If we're lucky, we might be joined by the love(s) of our lives—the first, the second, and perhaps even the third.

There'll be people who remind us of what we don't want to be. Some departures will leave gaping holes, while others will go unnoticed or cause us to breathe a sigh of relief. The journey of life is a journey of joys, sorrows, greetings, and farewells. Some people leave footprints on and everlasting memories in our hearts. Success in life is not contingent on getting on with everyone, understanding them, or persuading them that our way is best, but on simply enjoying the journey.

This is important because the huge conundrum of life is that we never know when our destination will change, or when our trip will be over. As such, we must live, love, forgive, and always give our best. If we do so, we'll be left with only beautiful thoughts when the time comes to disembark.

This life is your adventure, and you alone decide where it takes you.

Who are the people on your "bus of life"? Which of them have left footprints on your heart? Think about them, then pick up the phone and call them. Tell them about this book and how it challenged you to think about the people you care about most.

- _____

- _____

- _____

- _____

- _____

- _____

- _____

- _____

- _____

- _____

- _____

- _____

- _____

- _____

- _____

- _____

Attracting the "Right People" into Your Life

The question of who will make you happy on your journey is one I cannot answer. To fill your environment with your preferred type of people on a long-term basis, I invite you to become one of them. It is then that you will begin to attract exactly this type of person into your life.

> This is because people like people who are similar to themselves.

It's also because people find few things more attractive than sincerity and authenticity. Can you guess what I'm about to say? Yes: it's time to take off the mask and lift your protective visor.

According to Dr. Brené Brown, who has reached more than ten million people with her TED Talk on the subject, vulnerability is the key to connecting with others. We often believe that as soon as we show our vulnerable side, people will no longer want anything to do with us. However, nothing is more captivating than strength combined with the honest communication of weaknesses.

Yes, dear reader, you can and must open your heart to make progress. Often, we feel uncertain about opening to others because we are afraid of what our counterparts might think about the less-than-perfect areas of our life—the ones we cover with a rug or shove under the sofa as soon as a person unexpectedly enters our lives. To show yourself as you really are requires a lot of courage, but in the best-case scenario it is rewarded two or three times over. When you are honest about the things that affect you and render you vulnerable, it makes you approachable and incredibly attractive to others. Instead of relentlessly policing and concealing yourself, I invite you to engage with others with a spirit of openness.

Vulnerability is not a weakness; on the contrary, being vulnerable is an oft-underestimated strength and a prerequisite for stable relationships. That this applies without restriction—even in the business world. The best leaders I've met in the last twenty years—those who rally a team behind them in times of crisis instead of taking the easy route and blaming senior management—are the ones who show their human side at company parties and concede their mistakes and weaknesses.

It is dangerous for us to suppress our vulnerability due to misguided embarrassment. We now know that all our emotions mutually influence each other daily and are constantly interacting. This means that if we deliberately attempt to conceal or suppress this vulnerability, the negative energy is inevitably displaced and, without us having any control over it, impacts our ability to feel happiness, joy, and love.

A few years ago, I attended a seminar in Thailand and had a chance to witness how beautiful people can be when they relinquish their external filters. As part of the session, we were stripped of the things we used to beautify ourselves to the outside world. For many women, it was makeup; for me, it was my hair gel and clothes.

At first, as I sat in my underwear with unwashed hair among a group of complete strangers, my inner voice ran amok. After some time, however, it occurred to me how beautiful everyone was—precisely because of their vulnerable, imperfect idiosyncrasies. I realized how often I outwardly build a façade to seem strong. To this day, I'm still working on removing my mask of vanity and connecting authentically with others. It's not easy, but I manage it a little better every day. Try it for yourself—you have little to lose but a lot to gain. What things do you personally use to build a façade to the outside world?

- _____
- _____
- _____
- _____
- _____
- _____
- _____
- _____
- _____
- _____
- _____
- _____

You will no doubt have heard the saying that you are the sum of the people with whom you surround yourself. Once you have read the lessons in this book, I invite you to undertake an honest reality check. Who is good for you? Who supports you in being yourself and achieving your dreams? On the other side, who is an energy vampire? It is important to define this clearly because the people around you have an immense influence over your life. If you're not mindful about who you open the door to, it's easy to be undiscerning.

Have you ever noticed someone around you suddenly changes fundamentally as the result of a new relationship? I lost one of the happiest and most vivacious people I ever knew to a relationship with an energy vampire. Constant chipping wore away the stone and, over a period of years, this person became someone I barely recognized. Again: we become the people we spend our time with.

We protect our homes from burglars and install software that prevents our computers from getting viruses, but how do we protect the most precious thing we have? The simplest and simultaneously most vivid metaphor I can give you is lip balm. Your lips do not question the type of lip balm you use and whether it is organic or carcinogenic; they simply absorb what you put on them and distribute the substances— healthy or harmful—into your body.

"What's the solution?" you might be asking.

It's quite simple: you must surround yourself with people who are on the same "life mission" as you. What kind of people do you want to see in your environment? What are their character traits? What values do they live by? How should they behave?

At this juncture, my advice is: look at the qualities you have listed above, then become one of the people you have described. As you do so, you will automatically attract people who benefit you rather than robbing you of energy. Ask yourself what gaps you still need to fill to change the person you are into the one you want to be.

- _____

- _____

- _____

- _____

- _____

- _____

- _____

- _____

- _____

- _____

- _____

- _____

- _____

- _____

- _____

- _____

Thanks, but No Thanks

In retrospect, reflecting on whom I spent my time with was perhaps the most important step in my self-development over the past twenty years.

It used to be incredibly important to me to be cool. Even though I had never been cool myself, the idea was lodged firmly in my head.

I warmed up on Friday evenings in preparation for a whole weekend of partying. Once my world, weariness had been numbed with alcohol, and people who were otherwise incapable of showing their feelings had mumbled into my ear how much they loved me, my world was all right. Why? Well, this was an assurance of belonging, and to be quite honest, I was terrified of being alone. Others' opinions about my appearance and my views were incredibly important to me, and I disguised my lack of self-esteem with meaningless half-jokes and quips. I wore the clothes that others had chosen for me and always endeavored to blend in.

Despite all this, at some point, something inside me began to resist this mainstream. I don't know if you, too, have ever had the feeling of being somehow different from the people around you.

I found myself in a permanent state of confusion. Was I "allowed" to be different? What gave me that right? Who was I? These topics had always piqued my interest, and I'd read books on personality development from a relatively young age. I went to seminars and enthusiastically told my friends what I'd learned. I hoped with all my heart that we'd be able to grow together, and I began to try and convert them. Alas, I quickly realized that I'd been labeled a nutcase, a waffler, or a dreamer, and few of them shared my new view of the world.

Suddenly, I was thinking big. I was no longer allowing rules and conventions to be prescribed to me. I was no longer one of "them." I was the black sheep, and people began whispering behind my back. This was the beginning of the personal selection process in my life, and I made a list of the attributes I wanted in those around me:

What I was looking for:
- Big thinkers
- Doers
- A willingness to love
- Vulnerability
- Love
- Social engagement
- Holistic thinking

What I no longer wanted:
- Drama
- Resentment
- A victim mentality
- Whining
- Lies
- Gossiping
- Small-mindedness
- Hate
- Jealousy

Time for your list. What qualities do you want to see in the people around you, and where do you want to draw the line?

- _____
- _____
- _____
- _____
- _____
- _____
- _____
- _____
- _____
- _____
- _____
- _____
- _____
- _____
- _____
- _____

Today, I no longer have any desire to put on an act and surround myself with people who don't 100 percent fit my criteria. I did that for a long time, and one of the beauties of getting older is being able to say "no" without worrying about it. I can now recognize our shared moments as a gift and, at the same time, walk my own life path with a handful of people who have the same values and standards as me. For a long time, I aligned my life with the opinions of others, and this made me unhappy. Now, I'm thankful to spend time with people who are good for me.

At some point, the time will come for you to engage in difficult discussions regarding your new situation. When I look back, this step was the one that permitted me to be where I am today. One day, I scrolled through my address book and asked myself the following questions:

- Who is good for me?
- Whose conversation makes me feel inspired?
- Who isn't good for me?
- Who gives me energy?

Then came probably the most difficult step of all. I called up some old drinking buddies, chronic complainers, and energy vampires, and the conversations all went something like this.

"Hi, it's Tobi. I need to tell you something important, so please give me a minute of your time. It's been great to know each other, and I'm grateful for all the moments we shared. For a long time, we've been on completely different paths, and our priorities have completely shifted. Whenever I talk to you, I feel I'm dragging you into a world you don't want to be in and vice versa. I'm now in a phase where I'm working on my dreams and goals instead of drinking and partying. If you care even a little for me, I ask you to accept my decision."

These conversations were often incredibly difficult for me, and the next logical step was for me to move to another city to resist the temptation to fall back into old patterns. Even if it hurts, it's important to tell the truth. This includes: "Thanks for the invitation, but no thanks, I'm not going to come." I never go to events just out of courtesy because I have no time for that in the short journey we have here on this planet.

My best friend from school called me shortly before my wedding to say that he wouldn't be attending my bachelor party. He had nothing in common with the people who'd be there, he said, and he didn't get on with them. I was hurt initially, but I later came to be grateful for his openness. I had completely changed my environment, and my new environment had completely changed me.

Many people decide to pursue a different type of life: a safe life with a stable job. I fully accept that. Sometimes I wish I were like them, but I'm not. The question is, should I deny myself my dreams to be close to people I used to care about?

Relationships with Mentors

"A mentor is someone that allows you to see the hope inside yourself."

—OPRAH WINFREY

In a recent radio interview, I encountered a particularly interesting question. "If you had to start again from nothing," the host asked, "and if you were only allowed to keep one thing, what would it be?" At first, I didn't understand, so she explained further. "You can choose to keep anything from your current life: your team, your podcast, your newsletter, your social media audience, anything you want."

I didn't have to think for long. "My chosen item," I said, "is the address book with my mentors' contact details." Why? Because it was the help of these generous individuals that got me back on my feet in a couple of months, right when I needed it most.

Over the last twenty years, I've endeavored to meet a particular challenge: to offer added value to my mentors—that is, those people who are much further along my chosen path than me—without asking for anything in return. I want to credit their relationship balance, not deplete it. I prefer the motto, "Be so good that you're impossible to ignore," over the asinine cliché of "Fake it 'til you make it." Mentors can recognize phonies a mile off and are quick to distance themselves when they realize you're playing a part. Whenever you speak to a potential mentor, they'll be focusing on one all-important question:

Do I see myself in you?

- Are you a younger version of me?
- Are you prepared to pay a similar price as the one I did?
- Do I see a fire in your eyes and hunger in your belly?

If they can answer all the above in the affirmative, they'll automatically take you under their wing. No formal request is required, and such a request is inadvisable anyway since asking can signal low self-esteem. Far better to offer such added value that your mentor simply has no other choice—and to start from the first moment you meet.

It's fruitless to attempt to mooch your way from one influencer to the next. Instead, I advise you to engage potential mentors with two things: one, a question, and two, an offer that conveys your internal attitude: "What can *I* do for *you*?" Ninety-nine percent of the inquiries I receive are friendly, insightful, and appropriately self-effacing. Inevitably, however, some are not so positive—and these demonstrate perfectly how *not* to get me on-side. The story below is a prime example.

A few months ago, I was standing in front of a urinal, zipper down, and welcoming the chance to relieve myself after three hours of travel. Before I knew it, a man was hitting me on the shoulder. I rocked forward. "Hey," came a cigarette-laden voice in my ear. "You're pretty big now, right? I make health products—I'll leave you a sample."

By the time I was able to react, it was too late: a hand had tugged on my unzipped trousers and stuffed an item into my pocket. After leaving the toilet, I reached inside and found a business card and product samples. Take it from me, friends: this is *not* how it works. Relationships are not one-sided affairs.

If you want to gain a mentor, I recommend you prepare answers to the following three questions and know them off by heart. You should be able to reel them off after a party at four in the morning, or by the time the lift arrives at the fifth floor:

- How does the mentor benefit from the fact you exist?
- What problems can you solve for the mentor?
- How do others benefit from the fact you exist?

To illustrate what I mean, I want to tell you the story of Justin.

Over a period of weeks, we received a variety of speculative applications from Justin, who had hopes of working as a videographer at my firm. We had too many applicants to give everyone a chance, so we sent a polite rejection. We had no way of knowing whether he would be valuable to us. But that wasn't the end of the story.

A few weeks later, I was staying at my favorite hotel in Hamburg when I received a call from reception: "There's a package waiting for you here, Mr. Beck." This was not an unusual occurrence—I receive mail from creative applicants almost weekly. Justin, however, had waited for an especially favorable moment: after realizing I was spending off-time on Instagram, he'd handed the package over to hotel staff. The contents left me genuinely speechless. For weeks, Justin had been raking the archives for footage of me and crafting it into creative edits. "Do what you want with this," said the accompanying note. "The rights to it are all yours." As you might expect, we contacted him the next day and offered him a place on the team.

Prepare, pick the right moment, and approach situations without expectations: this is the formula for success. Show your worth, show your worth, and show your worth once more. If you succeed in doing so, others will willingly take you on their journey.

Balancing the Relationship Books

The principle of balancing, which is self-evident when it comes to banks, is a little harder for us to grasp in our own relationships. For me, a relationship is like a bank account. "That's not very romantic, Tobi," you might be saying. I know, but it makes sense, so give me a chance to explain.

Just as with a regular bank account, you cannot withdraw from a "relationship account" if you have not paid anything in. Logical, right? However, you can certainly try—and there are many relationships in which you'll get away with it, at least for a time. At some point, however, just as with your regular bank, it will be payback time. I don't know how willing you are to get into debt and max out your overdraft, but "free money" is never free; eventually, it catches up with you, compound interest and all.

How might we apply this to our relationships? Well, if we deplete a relationship account by withdrawing more than we pay in over a long period, one day, the owner will simply no longer be there for us.

Of course, there will be phases in which we withdraw more from a shared account than we pay in—that comes with the standard ups and downs of life. However, if we repeatedly fail to balance the books, we should not be surprised if our relationships deteriorate. What's more, I'm not only talking about romantic partnerships: all our relationships have this continuously changing balance from which both can withdraw and into which both can deposit. It applies to business relationships as well as friends and family.

Daily, I see many relationships that are ailing, and it is usually quite easy to discern that when it comes to the relationship books, there is an unbalanced plus-minus story. One partner gives more than they take, and the other takes more than they give. This is an unhealthy system and is not sustainable in the long term. Now, think about whether the accounts you share with important people in your life are balanced. You might even ask them directly what *they* feel and make sure that you pay off any debts.

It doesn't matter whether you do this using the five magic languages (which we'll discuss shortly) or by other means: the important thing is that you both agree that the bottom line is healthy. To this end, it is vital to communicate. If you think you might be taking too much, ask your friend how they feel; if you feel you're giving more than you get back, ask to schedule a chat soon. In some cases, you might find it useful to formulate your thoughts in a letter. The important thing is that you don't come with general reproaches but focus the discussion specifically around your feelings about this imbalance.

This is because, if there's one thing you can be sure of, it's that no one is able to read your mind. In relationships, you must be able to articulate what you perceive, how it feels to you, and what you would like to be different. This is the only way to create a dialogue without reproach, offering others the opportunity to change things. We all maintain a multitude of relationship accounts. As such, it is natural and perhaps inevitable that we will sometimes be the ones taking too much—and that our friends will gently inform us of this. Both people have responsibility for the joint account.

Which relationship accounts have you overdrawn, and into which do you think you pay more than you take out?

- _____

- _____

- _____

- _____

- _____

- _____

- _____

- _____

- _____

- _____

- _____

- _____

- _____

- _____

- _____

- _____

- _____

The Code of Honor

Most business and personal relationships break down because expectations are not met. This, in turn, leads to a state of frustration. You know the feeling: when your brain constantly nags at you that an acquaintance could have reacted better, or when it takes it upon itself to dwell on what you thought you deserved. Often, we are simply disappointed and annoyed, yet we usually don't say how we feel. How can this be avoided? In my view, the secret formula for happy, long-lasting relationships is a jointly defined code of honor—or, to put it more bluntly, rules. Relationships need rules for when people cross boundaries. On my first day the Wuppertal fire brigade at the age of eighteen, I quickly got to know the most important rule of all:

"We never let a comrade down."

What does this mean? Well, when I go into a burning house with my colleague, we don't leave unless it's together. Being in the fire brigade was about so much more than heroic missions and flashing sirens: at its heart, it was about honor. Many institutions deploy honor as a unifying force against unnecessary deliberation, the military and civil defense being obvious examples. But a code of honor only works if it is supported by all—and if disregarding it comes with consequences. In my time at the fire brigade, I was once required to scrub an ambulance with a toothbrush because I'd said something stupid in a moment of stress. I need hardly mention that this punishment took place outdoors in freezing winter temperatures. Repercussions are sometimes needed.

I've since become a great advocate of establishing shared rules. Naturally, my team, which operates like a family, has its own code of honor. Whenever a new member joins, the code is explained as a matter of priority, including the consequences for violating it. Since scrubbing with a toothbrush is not an appropriate measure for a decentralized, virtual company, we settled on social work instead. Whether baking cakes for a kindergarten or playing Christmas carols in an old people's home: everyone gets involved, from interns to the owner. Otherwise, there's no point. Once you are tempted to break the rules, you may as well never have set them in the first place.

Together, we set out the following values:

Punctuality

There are few things ruder than stealing people's most valuable resource: time. That's why we always have every team member in the room at least ten minutes before the start of a meeting.

Being Present

In the age of smartphones, it's rare to pay unconditional attention to those around you. That's why, during our meetings and meals, nobody is permitted to look at their phone. We always focus fully on the people we are talking to.

Respect

We're a diverse lot, and our differences are precisely the reason we work so well together. This means respecting others' opinions, even if we disagree.

GTTP—Get to the Point

As you should now realize, I'm not a fan of wasting time. Enter: "Get to the Point." By avoiding long, drawn-out, and unnecessary talk, we solve problems instead of creating hot air.

100 Percent

No matter which project we're tackling, we give it our all or not at all. This provides an ideal segue to my private life, where my wife Rita and I also share a code—one that's far more important to us than any paper or contract. Imagine you're on the plane before take-off and you hear the voice of the pilot on the overhead speaker. "Ladies and gentlemen: today, we're going to carry out an experiment. We're going to run the turbines on 99 percent only and see what happens as a result." What would you do? Get off? Me too.

In the same vein, people will be compelled to cut ties with you if you're no longer bringing your all to the relationship. I know many couples who have allowed their efforts to lapse, and the separation is not far off. No one wants a travel companion who's left the handbrake on. What's more, it doesn't even make sense to do so since full-on commitment is far less tiring than 99 percent.

Don't believe me? Sit on the sofa—not completely, but about half a centimeter above the surface of the seat. Ninety-nine percent can be arduous, right?

Social Media Relationships

May your life be as amazing as your social media profiles make it seem.

Have you lived today? By which I mean: have you lived your best Instagram, Facebook, Twitter, or other social media life?

Sometimes, I wonder what would happen if I didn't have social media. What would happen if I didn't post photos every day? Somehow, I'd feel I had only half-lived—or had lived only once, instead of twice like the other days. This is because our social media lives are quite disparate from our real ones: the lives that exist behind the filters, soft focus, perfect crops, and witty quotes.

Friends: if we are not careful, we—and certainly our future generations—will completely forget how to build authentic, healthy relationships in the real world.

Nowadays, our communication is based more than ever on social networks and messaging services. Indeed, even our selection of partners increasingly takes place online—and the choice is overwhelming. Big nose with a doctorate, blonde with a high school diploma, or a full-body tattoo with both? I've been out of the dating game for a long time, but from what I can see, it's akin to choosing a partner from a mail-order catalogue. Admittedly, they're not yet delivered with a fourteen-day return policy—but reader, give it time. We're only just beginning to see what a social network-centered world might look like.

Never have we had such an endless supply of apparently "perfect" people to choose from, all of whom we can network with across the globe in seconds. Yet friendship is something that takes time, something whose meaning we must explore in our interactions with others. It is about trust, shared values, and magical moments that connect us—often for a lifetime.

By contrast, friendship in social networks is accepted with a single click—and deleted just as quickly. Our notions of friendship are clouded by an entirely different understanding of the word: one that should be kept entirely separate. Likes have long functioned as virtual hugs. In 2016, researchers conducting a social media study at the University of California found that likes on social media activate the reward center in our brain. The scientists put people through an MRI scanner, showed them pictures with likes, and found that the same brain regions are activated as in other activities that make us happy, like eating a piece of chocolate, having sex, or otherwise feeling joy. Isn't that a little unsettling?

When we get likes for our posts, messenger substances that make us happy are released in the limbic system, the reward center of the brain. Because our brain enjoys being happy, it seeks for us to repeat these actions regularly. This suggests that positive reactions to our social media activities hold a certain potential for addiction. For us as humans, the attention and feeling of validation are so satisfying that we crave them again—and again and again. What's more, this form of validation is quickly available, even if we're feeling down in the moment. Snap a quick selfie, apply a sunshine filter, and a surge of digital dopamine won't be far off.

Many of us wake up in the morning and check our emails, our likes, and our friends' status updates before we get up. Ironically enough, we do this to feel connected with others. What's more, we already know that if we repeat something enough, it soon becomes "normal" for our brain.

Yet, this one-dimensional contact with our environment causes us to miss out on so much. Most of all, it causes us to forgo real-life contact with the people behind the screens: the versions that exist in real life, not the filtered ones that imply perfection. There are people on my social networks whom I wouldn't recognize on the street. The editing magic that was once reserved for Hollywood stars can now be downloaded at the press of a button: "fake life to go, please." With all this in mind, can we be surprised that we're no longer capable of forming genuine relationships, let alone maintaining them?

Moreover, how are our children to recognize that this virtual life is not reality? From experience, you might say—but then, from what experience? Even we, as adults, sometimes find it tricky to look behind the facade and remember that social media isn't real. Ultimately, all of us are guilty of pretending to live perfect lives, comparing ourselves to an illusory world that does not exist. Quite a tricky situation, isn't it?

On the one hand, it's not tricky at all since we logically understand all the above. On the other, do we trust ourselves? Do we not sometimes fear, subliminally, that everything *is* better for others, that it isn't the filter making it look that way? Which of us doesn't, on occasion, have the feeling that much of other people's lives is perfect, and it's a shame that we can't do it that way?

Now, don't get me wrong: I'm not saying that social media *isn't* a great networking tool. Among other things, it helps me reach people who would otherwise not have heard of me. It enables my crew to easily arrange *Bewohnerfrei*[1] sessions with a wide variety of people, and thus to bring together individuals who think the same, have similar notions of life, and share a drive to succeed. We use social media channels to come together and celebrate what's behind the screen.

We must never lose the ability to examine what defines us: who we are behind the profile. What remains when the filters are gone—what makes us human, connects us with others, and is so much more awe-inspiring than any form of Photoshop. Our value cannot be measured in likes alone.

Stop comparing yourself to others.

Above all, remember: the beauty of another life doesn't diminish the beauty of your own. For one thing, you never know what's behind it. My experiences over the past few years have shown that often, the grass is only greener on the other side because it rains *all the time*.

Re-establish proper relationships with those around you and take time to ask them how they're doing. After the first "fine," ask again. Ask

---

1 *Bewohnerfrei* is my podcast (German language) for ambitious individuals seeking to rid their lives of energy vampires. To find out more, see: https://www.youtube.com/BeckTobias.

again and again—as many times as you need for your counterpart to realize you're not just making empty small talk. Then comes the difficult part: listening to what your counterpart is telling you. Spoiler: we've done our best to unlearn this skill, too.

On social media, we are solely in control of our sending and posting. We are the ones who determine when and where we virtually consume our social contact—that is, only when it suits us. An inconvenient message? No need to answer immediately: the text or voicemail will wait until we have time. Now, this has great advantages in terms of allowing us to plan our day in a self-determined fashion, but it also has a major disadvantage. Why?

When we interact directly with others, we are required to respond and be empathetic—on the spot, not once we've had time to think it over. When we interact directly with real people, we train our ability to interpret facial expressions and gestures. As a result, we can pick up and give back infinitely more than is possible with any messaging service.

With our smartphones, we feel more connected than ever before and simultaneously more alone. This is because the only things that *really* bond us are shared emotions and shared moments—not the ritual morning checking of 1,000 new likes. When we look back on our lives in our dying breaths, such moments are the only things we have left. I've never heard of a dying person who wished they'd sent more WhatsApps or retouched more selfies. By contrast, many of us end up regretting our lack of time with loved ones. Shared moments can't be collected on our smartphones but must be experienced live and in color. They happen during a backpacking holiday through the Himalayas, a barbecue in the garden, or a nice glass of wine together on the balcony.

Are there people whom you consider special, yet you only ever communicate with them in comments and likes? Are there people with whom you've longed to make memories but somehow never found the time? Make a note of their names and call them today. Rediscover the art of real-time communication and arrange a catch-up.

- _____
- _____
- _____
- _____
- _____
- _____
- _____
- _____
- _____
- _____
- _____
- _____
- _____

What's More Important: Winning New Customers or Taking Care of Old Ones?

A complaint I often hear is, "My partner left me, but I didn't do anything." At this point, I think: "Yes—there's your answer." After having fallen in love with the man or woman of your dreams, you can't expect to get lazy after the honeymoon period and have everything remain the same.

I've worked for Walt Disney, and I don't subscribe to the notion that Disney gives us unrealistic visions of love. Rather, Disney films come to an end when the glitzy, confetti-filled phase is almost over; when the prince and the princess have found each other, dazed and dumbfounded by the cocktail of hormones in their brains, and are grinning maniacally into the camera, "The End" emblazoned across the screen.

"The end of what?" you might ask, as a critically minded viewer. You'd be right. This is not the end, friends; on the contrary, this is the beginning of their love. If the couple fails to pay close attention to the state of their relationship, if they slip into an arrangement like the couple shown here, there is a good chance that the supposed "happiest day of their lives"—their wedding—will truly end up being the pinnacle. Everything will be downhill from there, right down to the all-out bedroom screaming match. So much for the happy couple.

The surge of happiness hormones that has us floating on cloud nine at the start of a relationship decreases steadily over time. At some point, we stop seeing our union and partner exclusively through rose-tinted glasses—a good thing, since we'd quickly drive others mad if we didn't. But it's up to us whether we resign ourselves to the biscuit crumbs in bed, seek a new thrill, or endeavor to keep the relationship alive. The next chapter will discuss how we can keep our happiness hormones flowing with a long-term partner. We cannot change the predetermined course of nature, but we have the power to decide whether to accept it.

In practice, this acceptance is analogous to the change in how a business behaves once a customer is secured. Think back to any time you've signed a mobile phone or internet contract. (A few decades ago, I had a meteoric career in telecommunications sales, and I know exactly how these things go.) As long as your signature is not yet on the dotted line, you'll be promised the earth: free music downloads, a partner SIM for your loved one, and the original smartphone cover (made from authentic Kobe leather, of course). "How does that sound?" If you're *still* hesitant, a multi-function KitchenAid, a lawnmower, and a voucher for a foot massage will be thrown in.

Finally, seduced by all the extras, you tentatively scrawl your name. Three weeks later, you have a network problem. You call the customer service team, but this time, things are quite different. Unlike the sales rep who sold you the deal, this person's nerves seem to be rather jangled. They are uninterested in solving your problem, even less so in compensating you for the inconvenience. As soon as you sign your name, you become a regular customer: fewer free gifts, more waiting on the line for hours with an annoying automated voice. You are repeatedly transferred and put off, yet you persevere for days, fueled by the hope that what started so well cannot end in disaster. Have you ever experienced this? Hopefully, it was only from your telecommunication provider (many are guilty) and not from a relationship.

Don't create "holding music" for your relationships.

This doesn't just apply to romantic partners: long-standing friendships, sibling relationships, and business partnerships can all be put under strain by this unfulfilling holding pattern. We take each other for granted and believe that a good-natured "Please stay on the line" is enough to keep the other person happy. When was the last time you saw yourself visibly age while waiting in a service line?

Preserve this feeling and remember it whenever you're tempted to switch your own relationships to "existing customer mode." We all know what this looks like: another bouquet of birthday flowers from the petrol station on the way home (who doesn't love the smell of exhaust fumes, after all?), or a pair of socks and a six-pack of boxers from the TJ Maxx sale.

"But Tobi," you might be saying. "The day-to-day struggles of a relationship... You said it yourself. What about the hormones?" Yes, day-to-day struggles and fluctuating hormones are something Rita and I experience, too, but we refuse to let them define our relationship. The biscuit crumb bedroom scenario is *not* an inevitability. Wake up and take control!

Even if a relationship has been well and truly buried in the existing customer file, it's possible to extract it again. Admittedly, not every single time—but hopeless cases fall into one of two categories: Either they won't bother reading this book, or they're people in your own life, in which case you'll know from the chapter "Thanks, but No Thanks" that it's time to say goodbye.

How do Rita and I manage it, you ask? Over the next few pages, I've gathered the best, often personally tried-and-tested tips to avoid you becoming lax with your own customer care. If there's one thing you should never forget, it's that people can choose to stay on your "life bus" forever, or they can just as well choose to get off at the next stop.

Staying in "New Customer Mode"

Your Partner Is Always Number One

The daily grind, hormones, professional strain, children, sick parents, the dog, the cat, the dirty dishes… Our lives are wild and colorful, and there's always someone or something competing for our attention. Sometimes we forget to prioritize effectively and instead simply work through what has moved up the list by stealth.

What we often forget in all this is that our partner should always be number one. They are our rock in stormy weather, the thing without which everything else would cease to make sense. If something comes up that is important to your partner, if they need you, or if you notice that they are slipping too far down your priority list, it's important to restore them to pole position. You can postpone appointments and do the dishes later—trust me, they won't run away. It's much healthier to prioritize the sharing of moments—moments in which you show one another your mutual appreciation and which will pass unnoticed if they are not consciously lived.

I Love You as You Are

Do not try to change your partner; rather, remember the character traits, idiosyncrasies, and mannerisms that made you fall in love with them. Focus on these endearing qualities and tell them how much you love them. When people get praise and recognition for something, they willingly keep doing it without having to be asked. We take this very much to heart with our children, so why not with our partners, too?

Behave as You Did at the Start of the Relationship

At the beginning of a relationship, as we attempt to seduce our partner with metaphorical KitchenAids and lawnmowers, we are endlessly creative, sometimes even hopelessly romantic. We write sticky notes with effusive messages, though we usually struggle with words. We pick flowers through the pain of a herniated disc; we cook a steak medium-rare though we're vegetarian; we grin and bear our hay fever to camp under a starry sky. What a time to be alive.

These memories are a relationship gold mine. Bring the magic back to life by sharing things you experienced during the first throes of love.

Ultimately, you can't brush your teeth five times a day from January to June, then not at all from July to December, and hope that things will average themselves out. If you do, the only thing you'll end up with is a toothless mouth. Similarly, relationships are not static events. They require constant loving gestures, the nurturing of rituals, the frequent sharing of moments, and a lasting sense of mutual appreciation.

Rituals

Don't Shy Away from Making Commitments

As strange as it might sound, it's a good idea to sit down and write your own relationship code of honor. Rita and I have such a code. I don't want to reveal too much at this juncture, but if there's one thing I want to stress: smartphones, tablets, TVs, and game consoles have *no* place in your bedroom. The only film stars in the bedroom should be you.

The Fourth Flight from the Top of the List

Rita and I love our rituals. Once a year, we pack our bags and go away for a long weekend, just the two of us. Since we're globetrotters anyway, we don't hand-pick a destination: we drive to Frankfurt airport, walk to the display board showing the flights for the next three hours, and take the fourth flight from the top.

Sometimes, we get lucky—like a few years ago, when we landed in Kuala Lumpur thirteen hours later with sunshine and temperatures of thirty-five degrees in the shade. Sometimes, like the following year, we stumble off the plane fifty minutes later into the rain and ask ourselves what karma is trying to tell us. You need to love your companion a great deal to spend three days in a concrete jungle in November. But we do love each other, and the experience was worth it for the story.

"Anything-Is-Possible" Tuesdays

I adore this day. You can assign this to be any other day of the week. Alternatively, you can set a day where one of you gets to decide (almost) everything: what is cooked and who is cooking, whether you eat pumpkin soup and homemade bread cross-legged in front of the fireplace or your favorite home-delivered burger and truffle fries by candlelight in formal attire. You decide whether you go to the opera afterward or cuddle up on the sofa—and if the latter, whether it's with *The Crown* or *Ice Age 4*. The opportunities are endless.

Celebrate *Everything* with Your Partner

This is my favorite ritual. Whenever I achieve something I'm proud of, my first instinct is to tell Rita and share my joy with her. Of course, I also celebrate with my team and friends, but Rita is an immutable part of my success. At the end of the day, my successes are hers and vice versa. We are a team, and without her, I would never be where I am today. If there's one thing I urge you, it's to never overlook your partner's share in your success. Your mutual gratitude is worth endless celebration.

A Joint Vision Board

Another important ritual in our relationship is our shared vision board, which Rita and I create afresh each year. What do we want? What are our common goals? Have we set individual goals to ensure we do not lose ourselves in the "we"? For example, what do we both want for our children?

We write, paint, cut pictures from magazines, and make collages to inspire our specific goals for the coming year. If we achieve one of them, we celebrate properly. Sometimes, when we create the vision board, we think about how and where we plan to celebrate. It's not about carrying out everything on the board in a rigid, prescriptive fashion; rather, it's about getting creative, thinking about what you want, and visualizing your dreams for the year so you don't lose sight of them. Once these wishes are down on the board, it's a short mental step to tackling them. Bora Bora has been on our board since December, and that's why we're flying there in April. Cut it out, stick it on, do it.

Show Emotions—and Plenty of Them

Be Vulnerable

The more vulnerable you are, the better your relationships will be. You don't always have to be strong; in fact, your weaknesses are what make you unique and loveable. Involving your partner in the things that hurt you or make you feel stressed engenders trust, closeness, and a deeper mutual understanding. If you struggle to find time for this in the hectic daily grind, set aside regular breathing space to talk about the things that concern or worry you. These feelings must be allowed space in your relationship; otherwise, they will consume it.

Say Sorry

We all make mistakes. We are all sometimes moody and unreasonable. We're only human, and if we apologize sincerely and refrain from hurting with intention, this should not be something that drives us apart. On the contrary, it should bring us closer. Talk about yourself and your feelings. Learn to apologize and acknowledge the part you played rather than engaging in counteraccusations and blame-shifting.

Forgive, Forget, and Let Love Flow

If you accept a well-meant apology but continue to ruminate on the past, it gains an undeserved power over your relationship. Accept apologies and learn to forgive. Forgiveness is a wonderful gesture, primarily for the forgiver themselves.

Thank Your Partner for Sharing Their Life with You

Never forget that every day, each of us has a fresh opportunity to choose the person with whom we wish to spend our life. If your partner wants to share their precious journey with you, this is an amazing gift. Thank them for that.

Understand Where Your Partner Comes From

Talk about your past to lay the foundation for a common future. It's important to understand who you and your partner are today, but it's equally important to understand the experiences, adventures, and crises that made each of you the person the other fell in love with. Share this knowledge. Only by doing so can you learn to understand and love each other's idiosyncrasies.

Self-Reflection

What Do *You* Want?

Be aware of what you want from a partnership—what is negotiable and what is not. Do you want children? How important is your career? Where do you want to live? Do you want to stay close to your family? Speak openly as a couple about all your ideas and hopes together, preferably at the beginning of your relationship. Renegotiations don't usually work.

Let Go

It's not always easy to selflessly grant your partner freedom and space to breathe. This is particularly difficult if you have already had the experience of abandonment—maybe in childhood by a parent, previous partner, or another person close to you. Having someone leave us is one of the most painful experiences there is, and many people must relearn how to trust and feel safe in their next relationship.

Ultimately, clinging onto your partner will only serve to push them away—the opposite of what you want to achieve. Whenever we restrict a person and do not allow them the space they need, they will attempt to take this freedom by force. Pressure always creates counterpressure. Give your partner freedom—only then will they voluntarily come back to you, and it is only by doing this repeatedly that we learn that it is true. This takes a great deal of effort and self-discipline. Share your feelings with your partner. If they understand what unsettles you, they can better make sense of your reactions.

I Need You

Do you *love* your partner, or do you just need them? Dependency is not love. This is so infinitely important, and yet many people continuously confuse one for the other.

Don't get me wrong: a certain degree of emotional dependency in partnerships is normal and contributes to their stability. But if you feel you could not live without your partner's affection—and thus sacrifice your own needs in order not to be abandoned—things start to become unhealthy. If you stay with your partner merely to avoid being alone, to satisfy social norms, or to maintain a financial status, it's time to reconsider. The same applies if you find yourself asking, "Who am I supposed to be depressed with if not with you?"

Which of the things in this chapter occurred to you spontaneously?
Are there rituals in your relationships that prevent them from slipping
into the existing customer file?

- _____

- _____

- _____

- _____

- _____

- _____

- _____

- _____

- _____

- _____

- _____

- _____

- _____

Forever and Ever

A few years ago, I was booked on a ship as a freelance wedding speaker. These were the words I chose for the bride and groom:

Perhaps God plans for us to meet the wrong people before the right one so that when we meet the right one, we are extra grateful for this gift.

Love begins with a smile, grows with a kiss, and is sealed with a wedding in all cultures of the world, just as it has been for thousands of years.

Today and in the coming days, everyone's eyes will be on you; everyone will be wishing you love and happiness. But good wishes are only a piece of the puzzle. Love requires work, work, and more work.

After all this time, you should know each other's quirks, and if you really accept them "unconditionally," there's no need to worry about the future. Should dark clouds ever loom, I want you to think back to this moment.

I want you to remember this beautiful place, your partner's face, and all those around you who believe in your love and have traveled so many miles to be here.

Love means spending the whole day with each other on the patio without having to say a word—and feeling, when you leave, that it was the best conversation you have ever had with your partner.

Unbox Your Relationships

Understanding instinctively and trusting blindly are gifts so precious that they cannot be expressed in words.

Every day, young pearl divers dive day and night in the South Seas to find the precious treasure their grandparents talked about. It is a treasure this precious that you now hold in your arms.

It is true that we do not value what we have until we lose it, but it is also true that we do not know what we are missing until we find it.

Giving someone your love is no guarantee that they will love you in return. Do not treat love as a transaction; give it time to grow in your partner's heart.

Do not look for beauty; it is deceptive. Do not look for wealth; it is transient.

Look for someone to make you smile because one smile is all it takes to light up a dark day. You are lucky that you have found the one who makes your heart joyful.

There are moments when we miss others so much that we wish we could kidnap them from our daydreams just to hug them.

Dream together the things you want to dream; go together where you want to go; be who you want to be because you only have one life and one opportunity to do the things you dream of.

Never forget: your relationship is not a dress rehearsal.

Marriage does not grant access to a universe of guaranteed happiness but to a vast universe of learning. Grow together and be each other's role models.

I also want to share a further thought:

May you be happy enough that your marriage softens you; may you have enough challenges to make you strong; may you have enough sorrow to preserve your humanity; and may you have enough hope to bring you joy.

Try to walk often in the other's shoes. If you find them uncomfortable, it's likely that your partner does, too.

Never forget the many little things that have previously brought a smile to your lips.

The happiest people may not always have the best of the best, but they make the best of everything that finds its way to them.

When you were born, you cried, and everybody smiled around you. Live your life such that when you leave this earth, you are the one smiling, and others are the ones with tears in their eyes.

Happiness is revealed to those who cry, those who suffer, those who seek, those who live, and those who strive for it. Such people endeavor to give their best each day and to be there for each other, for they realize how important it is to appreciate those who cross their path.

Now, the big day is here. Many years ago, your parents greeted you as a baby: "Welcome to the world, little one!" Now, there's a new expression of love in the stars:

We belong to each other from the bottom of our hearts, forever and ever.

Introducing: Oxytocin

That cloud-nine feeling at the start of a relationship is thanks to a rather confusing cocktail of hormones: oxytocin, cortisol, dopamine, and adrenaline. On ice, shaken, stirred, or with an olive, all of this is rather irrelevant to the brain in this state. All it knows is that it has a lot of everything and that the mix is just right.

We dance on rainbows, conjure up sunshine in the November drizzle, perceive only positive vibes, and drive everyone around us completely mad. What's more, we don't even notice it because annoyance is not a positive vibe, and our hormone-addled brain is blind to anything else. For the not-so-loved-up around them, newly-in-love couples are (to be perfectly frank) nothing short of a nightmare.

One hormone that accompanies us through this first phase of a relationship is oxytocin, referred to by some as the "love" or "cuddle" hormone. Its role is to enable us to let one another in, behave empathetically and morally, and begin to build our love for a partner.

From the beginning, oxytocin has a pivotal influence on the bond and trust within a partnership. Peter Walschburger, a biopsychologist at the Free University of Berlin, believes that the greater the level of oxytocin at the beginning of a relationship, the more positively it will progress, and thus the greater its longevity.

Since oxytocin plays an important role in the birth and breastfeeding of a baby, new mothers have large amounts of it in their bodies. In their case, the role of oxytocin is not only physiological—it also promotes the emotional bond between mother and baby. What could be more intimate than a mother's love for her child?

Unbox Your Relationships

We know that large quantities of this cuddle hormone are released during the exchange of affection and that body heat also plays a role in the equation. Ever struggled to keep your hands off a new partner? It wasn't your fault: it was the oxytocin tango being danced inside. As we snuggle up and look deep into a lover's eyes, our hypothalamus fires off series of these "happiness molecules." (Thanks must also go to the pituitary gland, which distributes them liberally.)

When we're falling in love, it's easy to feel like that feeling will last forever. After our first big heartbreak, however, most of us are wise enough to know that this is not the case. Even those who are unaware of why this happens will know that "forever" can end much faster than we expect.

There are reasons for this, and they're not necessarily as obvious as "dirty socks" or "squeezing the toothpaste tube from the middle." Whether we like it or not, the level of oxytocin in the body gradually decreases the longer a relationship lasts. The hypothalamus slacks off, and the pituitary gland saves its few oxytocin particles for high days and holidays.

As a result, our relationships become unstable. We cheat on our partners, stumble over things that would previously have been invisible, and feel annoyed with things that once seemed insignificant. The *really* cruel thing is that this is what evolution wants.

After around four years, a relationship stabilizes, and we begin to find the balance between security and trust (on the one hand) and the desire for adventure and the unknown (on the other). Similarly, after four years, a child has taken its first steps toward independence and has less of a need for the constant care and attention of both parents. From an evolutionary biology perspective, this four-year period is easily explainable: for most of history, the care of both parents during these initial years was what most increased the child's chances of survival. After this intense initial period, our hormone levels don't revert completely back to their factory settings, but there is a noticeable drop in their happiness-creating effect. By the seventh year, most romantic partnerships have reached the following conclusion:

They no longer make the participants' hearts beat faster—unless, of course, they are divorce lawyers by profession.

At this point, you might say, "Fine—I'll do what evolution wants. I'll leave this partner and look for a new one." But does it make sense to start from scratch just because your hormones tell you to? It has been proven that when we feel unfulfilled in a long relationship, often what we need is *not* a new partner but the happiness hormones that initially connected us. Is it worth relinquishing your trust and love for that?

Of course, if your shared journey has come to a genuine end, there's no point staying on the same bus. But if you're both still headed along the same route, sharing the same values and pursuing similar goals, you should aim to get the oxytocin flowing again—or better still, not allow it to dwindle in the first place. And this is the easy part.

To produce oxytocin, a hug must last at least twenty seconds, so hug as much as you need to with your partner and your children. Cuddle your pets. Hold hands. Exchange affection. Have sex regularly. Relearn how to laugh together. Talk about your feelings. Compliment one another. Revel in happy memories and create new ones. Stare into each other's eyes. Surprise one another. Concentrate on the positive. Make time for old rituals. Create new ones. Learn your partner's language of love by reading the following chapter.

The Five Languages of Love

Some time ago, I read a deeply impressive book by American chaplain and marriage counselor Gary Chapman. Like the languages of the animals, which I'll go into in detail later in the book, his thoughts on communication in relationships contain a certain element of alchemy and magic.

Love can be expressed in many ways. As such, we shouldn't be surprised if we sometimes don't feel loved despite the presence of loving people in our lives. Perhaps these people are expressing their love in a different language, one we do not understand because we "speak love" differently.

In other cases, we may feel incapable of conveying our love for someone close to us. We become frustrated, unsure of what to do to help them understand their importance. Here, too, it may be the case that our love languages are misaligned. But don't worry, this chapter is going to change that.

According to Gary Chapman, there are five different languages of love. It is rarely the case that a couple speaks the same language, or that they prefer to receive love in the same way. This is not important. Instead, what's important are two things:

- Recognizing your own language.
- Learning to decode the languages of your loved ones—the people you want to feel loved *by you.* It's not about doing just anything for these loved ones but about doing the right thing.

1. Words of Affirmation

The first love language is words of affirmation. If you're one of those who speaks this language, you need frequent validation from your loved ones in the form of praise and recognition. You flourish when people compliment you—whether for your smile, your loving manner with kids, your career ambitions, or the Nobel-worthy resourcefulness with which you clean the bathroom. I don't know your specific talents, but I *do* know that genuine praise means more to you than anything else.

Words of encouragement are your motivation. They can awaken latent talent. They inspire you to perform at your best and afford you a sense of security: "I am loved."

If your partner speaks the language of words of affirmation, what can you do to show them your love?

Praise them. Focus on the positive. At least once a day, point out something you think they've done well. The "pro version" of this is to find something different every time. And if you can't even get started? Well, you should probably consider finding a different person to compliment... just kidding. It's normal to have to think or look carefully. It takes practice to speak a different love language, so don't shy away from making a little effort.

Don't allow resentment to fester. This applies to all relationships but especially to those where one or both partners speak the language of words of affirmation. Nothing is more painful to them than a past moment of discord that is endlessly rehashed. Next time you have a discussion, choose your wording carefully.

Write little sticky notes bearing the message "I love you." These work wonders. Hide them in a briefcase, a Tupperware container, a spice cabinet—anywhere your partner won't necessarily expect them and will find them when they're alone (that is, if they don't like a fuss).

Call them during their lunch break to say you're looking forward to seeing them or email them at work just to tell them you love them.

Encourage them to do something that's always been on their bucket list, whether that's a diving course, yoga instructor training, or poodle breeding.

2. Quality Time

The second love language is that of time for two, of shared moments. Many people misunderstand this as simply sharing space with a partner, but it's not enough for you to sit next to each other and read the newspaper (unless, of course, you sing the cultural section together, rap the sports results, or make a poem of the weather—and if this is your thing, don't let me stop you). As nice as it might be to relax with a coffee (or green smoothie) and each do your own thing, this doesn't count. No matter how healthy your breakfast is, your relationship needs vitamin "T": the nourishment of quality time.

Of course, being an intelligent person, you'll have understood that it's less about the time you spend together than about giving one another undivided attention. It's about taking part in each other's lives, reflecting on the previous day or the day ahead. The key is to relearn how to listen and be in the moment.

When a partner speaks the language of quality time, enjoying shared moments is particularly important for you as a couple. Here's how this could work in practice:

Organize a candlelit dinner at your favorite Italian place or take an evening stroll through the park. Attend a pottery course together, go to the theatre, spend a weekend at the Ritz-Carlton spa, or create a home spa with whatever you can find.

Once a week, plan time to focus on *just* the two of you. What's on your mind? What are the things you want to start doing together again? When the mundanities of everyday life are off the table (kids, work, etc.), you might realize how little else you talk about. High time to change that.

Make this time when your partner least expects it. Plan a spontaneous long weekend or a proper phone catch-up during a business trip. If it's snowing, pick your partner up from work early to go sledding with a Thermos flask of mulled wine or fruit punch in the car—delicious!

3. Gifts

The third language is the language of gifts. You might be thinking, "That could get expensive!" Not necessarily. If you speak the language of gifts, small gifts mean just as much as that long-lusted-after dress from Dior. The key is to give imaginative gifts that are lovingly chosen and meaningful to the relationship.

Perhaps a bottle of red from that little Provence winery could find its way to the kitchen table. The gift doesn't necessarily have to be valuable (though, of course, it can be). It might be extravagant to park a different Porsche 911 on your partner's driveway every week, but if you want to, don't let me stop you—sometimes a man needs a car to match his watch.

Incidentally, there doesn't need to be just one language of love for each person. My wife Rita's languages, for example, are those of gifts and words of affirmation. Whenever I'm on the road for a while, I bring her a gift that reminded me of her. Sometimes it's a magazine article or her favorite chocolate; sometimes it's a bouquet of flowers in her favorite color.

If your partner speaks the language of gifts, giving the right thing matters more than it does in other relationships. A few ideas:

Give with imagination. Often, the best gifts are the little things: an ice cream from their favorite gelato shop on a summer's day or a bouquet of flowers picked after a morning run.

Give something homemade: a story you have written, a picture you have painted, a photo album with shared memories, or a piece of jewelry made with a shell from your last holiday.

Keep a notebook of ideas or set up a list on your phone—a handy place to jot things down.

Get inspiration from friends. You don't need to come up with everything on your own. Perhaps your partner has expressed a wish to you.

4. Acts of Service

The fourth language is the language of acts of service. If this is your language of love, you'll place great value on your partner's willingness to support you. This support might come in the form of everyday acts: tidying up or making coffee in the morning. Other times, your partner might support a new business idea by keeping things off your plate during a stressful phase at home.

My love languages are those of acts of service and words of affirmation. I get happy about the little things, like seeing my favorite cup waiting by the coffee machine in the morning. When I come home from long training sessions or seminars, my favorite meal (Latvian pancakes) is often on the table, my shirt for the next day is ironed, and I don't need to worry about anything but spending time with my loved ones.

If your partner speaks the language of acts of service, what can you do to show them your love?

Once a week, take care of something they would normally have to do for themselves. Fetch croissants on a Sunday, pick the shirts up from the dry cleaner's, take the garbage out, walk the dog when it's your partner's turn, or attend their root canal appointment for them (all right, this one might be beyond even the most devoted partner). Any little act of caring will be appreciated.

Make a list of all the things your partner's been asking you to do. If they really speak the language of acts of service (and if you haven't yet mastered it), there are bound to be a few things outstanding. Start a project that needs attention: fitting the winter tires, renovating the bathroom, or even making over the whole house, depending on how much time you have.

Openly ask your partner how you could better support them. Even if you're able to come up with some things off the bat, this is the best and most successful way to learn this love language.

5. Physical Touch

The fifth language is the language of physical touch. If this is your language, you'll likely already know who you are. If your partner spends just one night away, you can kiss, cuddle, and stay awake for hours on the next. You need physical closeness, and every hug recharges your batteries. It might be one hundred degrees in the bedroom (and your partner might be praying for an icy drink), but you still want to fall asleep snuggled up. You don't care if your arm has serious pins and needles—you just want to be cuddling when you land in the land of dreams.

The affection you need can be multifaceted. You like it when your partner puts their arm around your shoulder or strokes your cheek lovingly, even when other people are around. For you, loving touches say, "We belong together."

If your partner speaks the language of physical touch, what should you do to make them (literally) feel your love?

Get used to exchanging affection when you say goodbye and hello: a kiss, a hug, or ideally both. A disinterested "Hi" or "See you soon" can hurt your partner much more than it can those who speak a different love language.

Hold hands in public again: on a stroll through the city, on Sundays in the park, or on a date night at the cinema.

Plant a soft kiss on your partner's forehead or on the back of their neck as you walk past (this depends, of course, on how you measure up in terms of size).

Surprise them with a massage. You could even take a course to learn from a professional.

Arrange a fixed evening during the week when you can snuggle up with a movie or just for a chat.

What is your natural language of love? Talk to your partner and discover the things that matter to each of you. Remember, it's not only your partner—your parents, friends, and children will also speak a certain language of love in their relationships with you. While your father might enjoy meeting up to play golf (and thus sharing quality time with you), your mother might prefer that you hug her or tell her you love her.

The languages of love play a role in all relationships; all you need to do is decipher them and learn how to speak them. Take it from me: the results will be magical.

- _____
- _____
- _____
- _____
- _____
- _____
- _____
- _____
- _____
- _____
- _____
- _____
- _____
- _____
- _____
- _____

No-Gos for Happy Relationships

All relationships are different. Some can only work if the gold-edged crockery is flung through the kitchen on a regular basis, accompanied by emotional outbursts, sobs, and make-up sex on the kitchen table. Everyone has different things that make them tick. If these routine outbursts of emotion "work" for you and leave your shared relationship account in the green, a few trips to the homeware store are a worthy investment. Couples' therapy costs more.

While there's no such thing as a "golden rule" that works for every couple, there are many universally applicable considerations. Relationship researcher and psychology professor John Gottman, who has spent decades researching the variables of fulfilling relationships, defined the following no-gos for happy couples in his book *The Seven Principles for Making Marriage Work*:

Criticism

It goes without saying that within a relationship, we need to be able to say what is bothering us and what we want to be different. Gottman does not question the "what;" rather, he is more concerned with "how" and "when." Accusations, complaints, and nagging—things that suggest your partner's inadequacy in your eyes—are toxic for your relationship. Take time to discuss things and formulate the things you want to change as wishes, not criticism. Talk about how you feel, not about what your partner has done wrong. "I" statements are a good starting point for this.

Scorn

Sarcasm and cynical comments can be the death knell for a relationship. A bad-tempered throwaway comment can hurt your partner deeply and stay in their memory, even if you quickly forget it. Nothing makes us more vulnerable than loving someone with all our heart, which is why we must pay special attention to how we express things when talking to our loved ones.

Self-Justification

When your partner talks about something that is bothering them, fight the urge to jump in and justify yourself. When you find yourself wanting to say "Yes, but...," take a deep breath and continue listening. Try to understand their point of view, even if it takes some work on your part. When criticized, most people's first response is to defend themselves and affirm their innocence. But it's not about apportioning blame; rather, it's about making sure each partner in a relationship feels loved by the other one. Acknowledging your partner's feelings and reflecting on what you (might) need to change isn't easy, but it pays dividends.

Walls

"Baby, we need to talk!" While women usually prefer to confront an issue, men are more likely to close themselves off. But silence doesn't help—as the male partner withdraws, the female partner feels alone and misunderstood, and in the long-term, the two drift apart. If something's bothering you, don't be scared to talk about it.

Other no-gos, from my own experience include:

Threats

"If you don't do what I want, I'll leave you!" Emotional blackmail has nothing to do with love and everything to do with an inability to achieve the desired outcome by any other means. This is not a basis for a relationship, and both partners must realize and accept this.

Not Asking for Help

Admitting to a problem and asking for help is *not* a sign of weakness. Tell your partner how they can help or join forces to figure out the problem. A person who loves you will usually notice that something is wrong, even before you tell them. Letting your partner share your problems is a sign of trust.

Nobody can reliably guess what we are feeling. On occasions, in a close partnership, we may be able to say things by saying nothing. When this happens, it can be a magical way of reaffirming the bond. But we should never forget that constant mind-reading and the silent divination of our needs are impossible in the chaos of day-to-day life.

According to John Gottman, each negative experience in a relationship must be balanced out with five positive ones. But don't you think it'd be better to avoid the negative ones at all? Talk to each other, or write letters, if you find it easier. Most importantly, keep the focus on you and how you feel. Refrain from engaging in accusations, threats, cynical comments, or reactionary self-justifications. Perhaps you could even include some of these commitments in your personal relationship code of honor.

I'm Not Sick,
I'm Just Single

Being single is *not* a disease. I know that for sure: I've googled it, and it's not listed in any diagnosis or classification system worldwide. I don't think that we, as humans, are made to dance through this life alone, but it's essential that we can be alone with ourselves if need be.

After a relationship, it's incredibly important to give your heart a little (or indeed, a big) break and to spend some time with yourself. Enjoy the things you sacrificed in the relationship or those your partner didn't like doing. Take time to reinvent yourself or to calmly reflect on why your shared journey ended. Go on solo trips, discover new things, take yourself out to dinner, paint your bedroom pink, or put a crate next to the bed—simply because you can. You don't need to "cure" the state of being single; rather, you need to celebrate it. Enjoy the things you went without for your partner's sake or the ones you only did when they weren't at home.

Often, finding oneself single can be a genuine stroke of luck. Why? Because stumbling from one relationship to the next removes so many of the opportunities we have to get to know ourselves. Bella DePaulo, a social psychologist from the USA, has written dozens of books about being single and blogs about single life on *Psychology Today*. According to her research, it is when people are alone that they make the greatest progress in their personal development.

Moreover, as a single person, you have the chance to discover how to bring roses, sunshine, and happiness hormones into your own life. You don't need a partner for these things; in fact, people often only realize what they are capable of when they find themselves on their own. Those who used to burn pasta water become star chefs; others who couldn't replace a light bulb become regulars at the hardware store.

DePaulo also found that single people are better integrated into their friendship groups and have more contact with siblings and parents than those who are in relationships. During our phases of singledom, we build stronger ties to those around us simply because we have more time to do so: holidays with the boys, spa weekends with the sister, visits to the park with the godchildren, or cruises and Sunday brunches with the parents.

Even if, at some point, you fall in love again (and thus your schedule once again includes cozy evenings on the sofa or Sundays in bed), these moments will be yours to treasure for life.

I've spent lots of time travelling and lots of time alone—times in which I searched for and found my "why." I shared moments with people who are now part of my team and who I know I can rely on through thick and thin. It was only through these experiences that I was able to let my amazing wife, Rita, into my life—and for that, I will be eternally grateful.

If you're currently single and happy, don't let anyone tell you that you're "complicated" or that there's something wrong with you. Get to know yourself, share quality time with the people you care about, and experience what it's like to be able to rely on yourself. Be secure in the fact that it's possible to enjoy your own company, that you don't always *have* to look for a partner.

One day, when you're ready, you may take this increased self-confidence and be open to falling in love again—not because you need a partner to be happy, but because you want to share your happiness with someone else.

Help Me—I'm a Wok!

The selection of potential "lids" is larger than ever before, but still—somehow—nobody seems to fit. Sound familiar? I know many single women in their early-to-mid-thirties, for example, who desperately want a partner. There's no good reason for them to be alone. They take care of themselves, have their feet on the ground, know their worth, and have the experience of one or two relationships behind them.

They have discovered the joys of single life and enjoyed them for a while. By now, they know the advantages and drawbacks inside and out, and they're starting to feel that they could do without them. They want a partner, their own family, someone who is there for them and participates in their life. Of course, this whole scenario also comes in a male variant: a prince looking for his princess. There are many interesting men and women looking for partners, and thanks to apps and social media, it's never been easier to find one. So why do some people find it so hard?

When I talk to the single women I know, a pattern gradually emerges. (The same applies to men, so male readers need not feel excluded here.)

Again and again, I hear the statement, "I don't know, it just never feels quite right." Here's the thing, single friends: almost nothing in life is simply "quite right." We're all compromising, all the time. So why, when it comes to love, does the prince on the white horse have to save the princess from her self-built tower, reverse park with his left hand, massage her neck with his right, recite poetry, smell of strawberries, and, to top it off, come home from a twelve-hour day looking like the cover of *Men's Health*? Granted, fairy-tale princes *can* do this. That's why they're called fairy-tale princes—because they only exist in fairy tales.

Similarly, for men seeking women, there is little room for compromise. The looks of a Victoria's Secret model, not only perfectly groomed and beautiful, but sporty and easy-going, even on a backpacking holiday in the jungle. Such a mythical creature will effortlessly juggle career, diaper changes, and the Sunday roast under one roof—and is always in a good mood to boot. That goes without saying, doesn't it?

But for now, back to our single women. While nobody would tell you to settle and abolish your standards, be mindful that applying them so rigidly is also a mechanism of self-protection. No real man—one with real corners and edges—will ever be able to meet your ideals. All things considered, it's an effective way of not getting hurt and keeping all options open—and making sure that you remain alone in the long term. Think about it.

In a similar vein, a single man with "high standards" can protect himself from (further) disappointment if he clings to the prospect of his so-called "ideal woman," pretends that men don't have feelings anyway, and bemoans that "she just wasn't right."

Of course, there can be other reasons why a clever, attractive pot has no lid. Often, it's that they repeatedly fall for the same type of partner. If you put such an individual in a party of 500 people, some are guaranteed to pick the one who'll treat them badly. They won't give a thought to the other 499, though any of them would have been a better choice.

For some women, it is precisely who is not there, does not pay attention, repeatedly cheats on her, or otherwise treats her badly that will attract her like a magnet and have the world laid at his feet. Of course, this phenomenon is not exclusive to women. If a man has not experienced this himself, he will likely at least have a friend who has—one who is constantly introducing the same type of girlfriend and whose friends are quick to foresee the impending heartbreak.

Why do these people allow this to happen to them, and why do they keep on picking the wrong partners? It cannot be that they *want* to suffer. Instead, I believe there is another reason: that, at some point, their inner magnet has calibrated itself unfavorably. This usually, though not always, happens in childhood.

As you'll recall from earlier in the book, our parents are the ones who show us what love looks like, and at some point this information begins to shape our inner poles of attraction. If this calibration process teaches you that you must "earn" love by being well-behaved and adaptable, you will likely draw these kinds of relationships into your life—ones in which you sacrifice your own needs for your partner's approval.

Perhaps you learned from your parents that loving means giving more than you get back (remember when we talked about plus-minus relationships?). In this case, you will likely seek out someone who likes to take and is reluctant to give.

I don't know your personal situation, but somewhere in your inner magnet, your vision of a prince (or princess) is pre-set. Inevitably, you end up with a partner who delivers your learned version of love. Think of it like a well-trodden path in the brain. You might sometimes notice that such people are not good for you, but you still fail to seek out something different next time.

Why is this pattern so tricky to break? Well, because our subconscious—the magnet—learns slowly. We fall for the same types and ideas again and again without meaning to. When we realize that a relationship is bad for us, we don't get out of it but instead, try to change it—like a bad rom-com. We want the turbulent drama to have a happy ending. *Surely*, we think, *after all this time and effort, things must be about to take a turn for the better.*

But since when have dramas ever ended happily? Simply, this is not a challenge you can defeat; it's just how it goes. People do not "change," and certainly not because you want them to.

The person you love has learned a different version of love than you, a different way of treating people. You cannot simply delete it. You will never be able to change this person, nor the pre-programmed ending to your shared story.

One thing you *can* do is to find a new beginning. Try a different type of man or woman; only then might the ending be different, too. Identifying who you are naturally drawn to doesn't mean it won't happen again, but you *will* notice it early enough to get out during the opening credits. You know how the story will end—you've experienced it often enough. It's time to re-calibrate—not your drama, not your problem (anymore).

A word of caution, however. It might initially feel strange when a person understands you, lifts you up, and makes you the center of their life. It might feel unnerving if they appreciate your weak points and reassure you that even despite them, "You are my hero." Maybe you've met such a person before and left them because you felt it couldn't be love. But this form of love is not wrong or second-tier; rather, it's a form of "right" that you don't know yet. Give people a chance. More importantly, give yourself a chance. Give yourself space to leave the well-worn path in your brain and carve out a new one. It will take time for you to recognize and accept this new kind of love, but perseverance and patience with yourself will pay dividends.

Sometimes, we have to practice *being loved.*

The Language of the Animals...

...has completely changed my relationships with others. Many years ago, I came to the realization that speaking the languages of those around me would enrich my own life journey immensely. Now, I'm not talking about Spanish, French, or Mandarin—the languages I'm referring to are much, much easier. We already know them on a subconscious level; we simply need someone to bring them to light. That's what this chapter is all about.

The fundamental idea is not entirely new. It wasn't devised by me, but by someone much, much smarter than me. I didn't invent the model, but I have, so to speak, developed it further.

In fact, the model was invented by the Greek philosopher and doctor Hippocrates in the fifth century BC. (I think I would have quite suited being a philosopher—sitting on a rock all day and thinking of ideas—but since my time is the here and now, I'm happy being a speaker.) Hippocrates is long dead, but his idea of the four humors inspired Galenus of Pergamon to develop his own teaching of the four temperaments or "human types." In this same spirit, I trust that Hippocrates won't mind if I reimagine some of his ideas for our time.

Anyone who knows me knows that I've always been fascinated by the world: I like to travel, I love nature, and I'm committed to cleaning up the oceans with "The Ocean Cleanup." That's why I chose four animals to represent each of the four human types:

Owl—Shark—Whale—Dolphin

Yes, I know; these aren't just animals. What each of them is about will be discussed later.

You don't need to be a genius to understand the concept, just thoughtful and a little curious. As soon as you can recognize each animal's language, you'll begin to see the people you know with completely different eyes. More importantly:

You'll start to communicate with them differently.

Then, suddenly, crazy things will begin to happen. Your insufferable colleague will bring you your morning coffee. The brusque bakery saleswoman will smile at you for the first time and begin to reserve three croissants, just in case. Your (usually) night-owl partner will happily prepare the breakfast table, whistling "La Bamba" and arranging a vase of tulips (freshly picked while walking the dog, despite the April drizzle). Things may not manifest exactly like this, but they'll be very similar.

The language of the four animals will also help you to communicate more successfully at work, assemble more effective teams, and better recognize and satisfy your customers' individual needs.

As you read the following pages, you will undoubtedly think of your colleagues, family, and friends with a smile. You may even experience a few revelations (no, you haven't failed as a parent because your daughter's room looks like a bomb site while her three-year-old brother color-codes his socks in the drawer).

First of all, this is life. This is how it's supposed to be. This is a good thing.

Which Animal Am I?

At the end of this book, you'll find a special gift: a test to help you find your animal combination. However, you don't need to know which animal(s) you are to learn the animal languages. If this is your first time hearing about them, I'd recommend you take the test *after* finishing the book. Take it from me: the process is highly enjoyable, and you'll be amazed to see how much better you understand yourself once you understand the animals, too.

Each of us is a mixture of the four personality types: whale, shark, dolphin, and owl. Rarely is a person purely one type, with 100 percent of one animal and nothing of anything else.

In this model, no one animal is "better" than any other. All four animals have their reasons for existing, with individual strengths and weaknesses. As such, they are all equally valuable. We all have a "gene" for each of the animals; however, they are not always expressed in equal proportions. The (relative) expression of a particular animal is determined both by nature and by nurture—the environment we grew up in, the niches we sought out, and the skills we had to develop in childhood to earn our parents' love and praise.

If one thing is for certain, it's that our experiences of early life play a large part in shaping our personality. Were you a confident child or a reserved one? What were your most well-trodden mental trails? What was the view from your childhood bedroom?

The four animals can be seen in all areas of life. As soon as you speak the animal languages of others, you can begin consolidating your relationships and getting more out of your shared journey. I've been working with this model for almost twenty years and have used it in several German companies, including Vorwerk and Bugatti. Here, all employees know their colleagues' animals and their own, and there are animal symbols on many desks to warn of certain characteristics or encourage people in for a chat. The model of the four animal types is by far the most popular in my repertoire.

Countless letters from clients have confirmed its applicability in practice: it has saved marriages, revived friendships, and set healthier standards for office communication. Great! Still, I am mindful that the human spirit defies blunt categorization, and as such, this book is intended primarily to serve not as a categorization tool but as a "toolbox" for better communication.

If there's one thing I can promise, it's that you'll never again be bored at a cash register, bus stop, airport, or family celebration, no matter how dreary it may be. In fact, family gatherings will become workshops for improvisational theatre. Suddenly, you'll recognize why certain people get on (or don't get on) with others, why certain topics always stir up trouble, and what role you must play.

Ready for a small language course à la Tobias Beck? Here we go! I wish you much enjoyment in discovering your animal personality.

The Whale

No whale is like any other. Just as there are around ninety species of whales in the sea, there are a wide variety of whales among your fellow humans. The only difference is that these live on land and have two legs. Because of this, recognizing whales by their external appearance alone is only possible for the most experienced. After reading this book, however, you'll have endless fun identifying them from their personalities.

Whales come to this planet with one simple question on their minds:

> "How can others benefit from the fact that I exist?"

This way of thinking brings many positive results, and the beneficiaries are mainly others. This, of course, means that you could benefit, too.

Let's imagine that you are new to a city and are invited to a party. Striking up a conversation at the buffet, you mention you're soon going to be moving here with everything you own: your dog, cat, mouse, and three chinchilla babies included. If you happen to be talking to a whale right now, you're in luck. So eager will they be to help that they'll almost drop the last salmon canape—the one they were intending to give you anyway. What's more, their offer is completely genuine. Whales *want* to help, they love to help, and above all, they are pro helpers.

A whale will consider all the things you've missed on moving day, and as you might expect, they'll bring *everything* you could possibly need: moving boxes, blankets, tissue paper, adhesive labels, and, most importantly, other whales. Yes, you'll see many other whales whom you do not know but who are nevertheless happy to help you. A whale rarely travels alone. Why?

Because people like people who are just like them.

As well as their own kind, whales love those they can help. If you tell a whale you're moving at eight on Monday morning, they'll be there bright and early at seven. "But of course," the whale would say. "I've got to unload the packing boxes from the minivan."

In addition to all the equipment and helpers, there will be provisions for the moving crew. The evening before the move, the whale will spend hours spreading butter, chopping salad onions, making cheese rolls for the vegetarians, preparing a fruit salad for the fruitarians, and conjuring up a hummus dip in the Thermomix for the vegans. They'll even stop off at the printing shop and copy the recipe for anyone who wants to try it.

Of course, whales must take care that their willingness to help is not exploited, but more on that later. First, let's look at some more of their characteristics.

Whales are herd animals. They are sociable, do not like being the center of attention, and gravitate toward taking care of others. For a whale, orienting its life primarily around "fun" would strip life of all its meaning.

And because whales are drawn to those who are like them, they even go on vacation to the same places. Where the conditions are *really* ideal, like on campsites, there are so many whales that it's akin to a mass stranding. Whales love camping. Why? Because there, they can do exactly what they'd be doing at home: cooking, cleaning, washing, and more.

Whales are in their element on the campsite or in center parks, where they can take care of the powdery mildew on their neighbors' roses, teach the kids across the street to swim, and hand out their show-stopping tiramisu.

In the evenings, whale men fire up the barbecue to make sausages for the whole neighborhood—but only after helping little Harry next door to mend his bicycle. With a schedule full of important meetings, Harry's father is preoccupied with the week ahead—and when it comes to bicycles, he has two left hands anyway. As you might already have guessed, Harry's father is *not* a whale. He's a shark—but plenty of time for them later. For now: how many of you have already mentally embraced your new whale tribe?

Let's imagine that you're first and foremost a whale, a genuine helper type. When you play Monopoly, you let others win and feel at one with yourself and the world. You're a stalwart in any situation. You patiently merge two lanes of drivers each morning and give each of them a friendly nod to boot. There's no hint of irony, no dangerous spike in blood pressure; that's just who you are.

In addition, you love a certain kind of movie, and you've always got the requisite Kleenex on the coffee table. *Love Actually*, *The Notebook*,

It's A Wonderful Life—a proper whale knows them all and has also seen the directors' cuts.

During my psychology studies, I learned that media institutions have long deployed the principle of the four types of people. If you're clever—and you are, otherwise, you wouldn't be reading this book—consider this: what kind of television ads would you run to appeal to whales?

First and foremost, it's about timing. A hit romantic drama series is prime whale territory. Just before the star-crossed lovers are reunited, a cut comes, and your whale ad begins. It's a highly emotion-driven affair with tears, laughter, bittersweet goodbyes. In the closing scene (complete with driving rain), the two protagonists fall into each other's arms with huge boxes of thank-you chocolates. "Thank you," they say, "for being you."

On Monday morning, 200,000 whales then obediently trek to the supermarket—even though the chocolate is not their favored type. A bit of a cynical trick, right?

The world needs whales. Whales hold communities together, and their steadfastness often serves as the buffer between other personality types. In the office, they are a haven of peace and a listening ear; in a family, they are a rock among waves; in a friendship, they are the friend who picks you up at four in the morning when you've drank too much and luck has forsaken you.

A whale's most important character trait—and the one I personally find most impressive—is its depth. In nature, whales can dive up to 3,000 meters and form long-term relationships with their mates. When a whale takes you into their heart, you have a friend for life with whom you can share your secrets. And you needn't worry about being betrayed—whales will treat whatever you tell them with the strictest confidence.

Car stickers are another whale favorite. "Baby on board," for example, will be emblazoned on the Volkswagen sedan in which the whale family—always adhering to the speed limit—drives to the theme park to wait in line for hours and sit on the teacups for three minutes. No matter: for them, the main thing is that the neighbors' kids enjoyed it. Spot a keyring with a teddy bear or a talisman around the neck? These could also indicate a whale on two legs. Whales love souvenirs, and an entire industry courts the favor of these emotional buyers.

I'm sure you already have an idea who the whales are in your life. Some of you may be whales yourselves; others may feel like whales in specific situations, because usually, we are not 100 percent one type. We are all combinations of all four animals, with one or two that dominate our character.

Who among your family, friends, or colleagues can you identify as whales? If a few names occur to you spontaneously, write them down now.

- _____
- _____
- _____
- _____
- _____
- _____
- _____
- _____
- _____
- _____
- _____
- _____
- _____
- _____
- _____
- _____

Unbox Your Relationships

The Shark

"Save yourself! The sharks are coming!" we shriek, justifiably, when this monster of the seas appears. It is not only whales that swim in our vast human ocean, but sharks, too: perhaps the most feared of all sea creatures. If you're unlucky, a shark won't just bite you but eat you, bones and all—and that's just for breakfast. An admittedly unpleasant start to the day.

Undoubtedly, many of you will already have noticed that whales and sharks are completely opposite types. While the whale lives by the question, "How do others benefit from me?" the shark turns this on its head:

"What am *I* getting from others?"

A completely different kettle of fish.

It is not only surfers and divers for whom a shark encounter can be most unwelcome—sharks in the personal environment can be difficult, too, especially if we have not encountered them before. But this chapter is going to change all that.

Let's return to the party scenario from the previous chapter. This time, you don't happen to meet a whale, but a shark. (This, incidentally, is relatively unlikely, since sharks don't usually serve their own snacks, but let's say they got lost there for the sake of argument.) If you now tell the shark that you are moving next week, they will wash down the last canape with a sip of champagne and say that they, too, recently moved: 250 square meters of loft, 60 square meters of roof terrace, a sauna, a whirlpool, and a koi carp pond in the garden. Only the designer furniture from Bali is still en route. As we said above: a completely different type of person.

But hey, maybe you were also planning to furnish your new, thirty-square-meter basement studio with teak chairs from Bali and a koi carp in your mini bathroom sink. In this case, you'll have the shark's undivided attention. And even though the shark took the last salmon canape, you can be sure they will already have ordered more ("The ones with the caviar—and a bottle of magnum too!" they say, with a casual gesture to the caterer.)

To retain your companion's interest for the length of a drink, you should speak "shark" and find a topic that makes you interesting. Yes, I'm almost certain the shark can recommend a moving company— after all, he plays golf and attends Formula 1 with the boss. But the shark is not interested in your moving journey; rather, they're interested in what they can get from sipping a glass of magnum in your company. You see:

The fish must like the bait; whether the bait likes the fish is completely irrelevant.

It's always a good idea to have sharks listed in your contacts list—if you're looking to recruit sharks into your personal ocean, applying the above principle is key. This is relevant in many areas of life, but especially, of course, in any form of marketing.

While a whale adores TV shows that touch and warm the heart, a shark will only know them by hearsay—unless, of course, they are the head producer. Let's imagine you want to advertise to a shark man or woman. Where would you place this advertisement?

Because you're smart, you would take your ad and place it in *Bloomberg Businessweek* or the stock market section of the *Financial Times*. For even better results, you might place it in a glossy magazine about cars, golf, or architecture.

Sharks are real people magnets, both personally and professionally. Despite their formidable personalities and not necessarily warm-hearted nature, they exert remarkable power over others. Have you ever felt compelled to win a stranger's interest, even though they initially showed you no regard? This intriguing individual was almost certainly a shark.

Sharks provide leadership, radiate natural authority, and, regardless of the situation, are always willing to act as decision-makers. Such individuals are vital to society. In fact, it's thanks to them that we're not still swimming around in the primordial soup, wondering whether two cells might be better than one. The shark makes a decision, sees it through, and deals with the consequences.

When it comes to making decisions, many people are wired in precisely the opposite way. They lose themselves in the possibilities to such an extent that eventually, they forget about the actual question. Naturally, the shark's capacity for cut-throat decision-making is extremely attractive to others.

Moreover, as you might expect, a camping holiday is less than appealing to our shark brothers and sisters. You're not likely to find a shark on a campsite—unless it's Harry's father from the previous chapter, who owns the on-site shop.

Instead, a shark has their own ideal vacation spots: St. Moritz, the Maldives, Saint Bart's, and the Hamptons. You can find sharks wherever the tone is expensive and refined—and where many of their fellow sharks can also be found.

We already know that people like those who are like them. Such luxurious vacation spots offer manifold opportunities for sharks to encounter their fellow kind: during a lomi lomi massage in the spa, in a luxury Bali resort, or glamping in a snow igloo under the Northern Lights. These locations and resorts know exactly what sharks need and want, and most of the time, price doesn't matter. Those who earn a lot also have a lot to spend, a principle that applies equally in the world of personal style. While whales prefer their fashion to be simple and unostentatious, the shark can be found in the world's most upmarket boutiques. Preferences vary from one shark to the next: an unmistakable logo for one, bespoke tailoring for another. Clothing doesn't have to be practical; expensive is enough, and the shark's taste is not up for debate.

In general, sharks spend a great deal of time on their appearance, so never be afraid to compliment them liberally—after all, which of us doesn't like a compliment? We all have a greater or lesser tendency for vanity, sharks are just a lot more upfront about it. As such, don't expect a casual, "Oh, I got it on sale." That would be more of a whale thing to say.

If you compliment a shark's shoes at a party, they'll tell you exactly how expensive they were. "Amazon frog leather," the shark might say, "hand-softened by indigenous tribes under the full moon." If you now want to score some points (because the shark is your new boss or because you want a personal introduction to the moving firm), you'd do well to avoid mentioning the dwindling Amazon frog population. Why? Well:

> Just like all the other animal types, sharks need validation and (positive) recognition.

This trait can be seen perhaps most clearly in whales, who earn abundant recognition just by being there for others. For sharks, things are slightly different. A shark would rather be recognized for their achievements, for the extraordinary things they have done and acquired in life. Most of the time, an appreciative "Wow, from the latest collection?" should do the trick. It's not as difficult as you think.

Wherever you are, you can reliably identify sharks by their uncanny ability to park directly in front of any door. No parking space? The shark will find one. Time is money, and Amazon frog leather doesn't take kindly to wind and weather.

A few years ago, I was a keynote speaker at an event organized by a large German insurance group. One attendee was an hour and a half late, an already somewhat tenacious move. Imagine my surprise when he drove up to the building, beamed his headlights through the window, strode in, and slammed the door. *All eyes on me, bitches; otherwise, I may as well not have come at all.* Sharks don't just walk into a room—they make an entrance. As a keynote speaker, it was up to me to incorporate this entrance seamlessly into my presentation.

"May I ask you a question?" I said.

"You may."

"How old are you, sir?"

"Twenty-one. Anything else?"

"Just one more thing." By now, I was seriously stunned. "How did you come to drive a Mercedes S500 at twenty-one?"

He laughed. "Well, because there was no 600. What do *you* think?"

An outrageous answer? Of course. But it is not up to us to admonish grown adults; rather, we must handle such situations wisely, without getting bitten. Moreover, we should never forget that each animal has its good sides, qualities from which we can benefit. To enjoy these benefits, we must accept the challenges and understand that they are part of the whole.

Sharks only respond to a certain type of language. If you speak to them in whale language—"Could you...?" or "Would it be possible...?" or "Do you think it would be a problem...?"—they'll be gone before you've finished your question and you'll have lost the chance to recruit a genuine go-getter into your life.

Before we get to the next animal type, take a moment to write down the names of sharks in your own environment.

- _____
- _____
- _____
- _____
- _____
- _____
- _____
- _____
- _____

The Dolphin

Have you ever tried to sleep with one half of your brain and stay awake with the other?

Try it tonight: close one eye and leave the other open. Imagine the possibilities—while one half of your brain is sleeping, the other can do your tax return. Actual dolphins have long since mastered this; not the tax return, admittedly, but this "one-sided sleeping" to stop them from missing out. While for them, it's mainly about steering clear of threats, dolphins on two legs are similarly restless. Perhaps they, too, have long since figured out the secret of one-sided sleeping—though, in their case, it has an entirely different purpose.

If a dolphin wakes up to see confetti lying around, it begins to have a sinking feeling. "Why so much confetti?" it says. "What have I missed?"

The explanation for this is simple. Where whales were born to help others and sharks were born to have others help them, the dolphin— no matter the time of day or night—has but one single focus:

"Where's the next party, friends?"

Dolphins invented confetti. And glitter. And balloons, amusement parks, shopping centers, and many other things that sparkle—things that don't always make sense but are always fun. Dolphins know how to enjoy life. If you ask a dolphin when and where the next party is planned, they won't understand your question because, for them, life is one big party. You can recognize a dolphin by the way their phone rings. It doesn't just sound a tone, it simulates a rocket launch, flashing, vibrating, and projecting a familiar set of pop music lyrics into the air. Most of the time, the dolphin phone is kept in a colorful case, often impractical due to rabbit ears or a rainbow-colored unicorn horn—but hey, it has personality.

When a dolphin attends a party, you can usually find them on the dance floor, behind the DJ booth, or acting as the impromptu emcee. If a party turns out to be quieter than expected, the dolphin's stock of anecdotes will always liven the atmosphere. They have an unparalleled ability not only to remember jokes but to ace the delivery.

Dolphins are self-deprecating by nature. They don't take the world or themselves so seriously. *None of us get out of here alive*, they think, *so why not have some fun while we're at it?* Naturally, the best fun is had with others.

Human dolphins enjoy the act of play and the company of like-minded individuals. Not so different, really, from their marine namesakes, who perform acrobatic tricks and have sex for fun with different partners. "Why not?" the human dolphin would say. "Variety is the spice of life."

Dolphins are always surrounded by others—in fact, if you'll pardon the pun, a dolphin in company is like a fish in water. The more people they have around them, and the louder and more carefree these people are, the more in their element the dolphin feels. Conventions and rules make little sense to them: instead, they cause them to feel restricted. They readily overlook such conventions and rules, though rarely with malicious intent.

Imagine you're planning a black-tie party, announced several months ago with great flourish and fancy. What will the dolphin wear? That's right: a red, sequin-spangled gown with a rose in their mouth and a neon feather boa around their neck.

When it comes to your upcoming move, try to recruit at least one dolphin helper to ensure that the mood will be right, the music will be good, and the energy will stay positive right to the end. As a precaution, recruit *three*: a bit of backup is always good since it's never a sure thing that a dolphin will turn up. They might forget or mix up the date, oversleep, or end up hungover. There are numerous possibilities. In the end, maybe your move simply clashed with a more enjoyable date.

Unfortunately, a dolphin-driven type is not the best when it comes to reliability. Because of this, for your dolphin friends, a certain measure of patience is required.

A party without work is always welcome, but in the dolphin world, work without a party is not allowed. If the dolphin does show up while you're moving, they'll probably only get there once the boxes are inside. And if these boxes contain flat-pack furniture? Keep the dolphin away. "Instructions?" the dolphin will say. "There were instructions? I had them a minute ago...where have they gone?"

But so long as the conversation is not about shelves, dolphins have much to teach about life. They know how to get the most out of every situation and are perfect improvisation artists, thanks to their storytelling flair. While other animals bemoan Mondays, dolphins positively relish them; finally, they can regale their colleagues with their outrageous tales of the past two days. If you listen to such weekend tales—which are endlessly entertaining, by the way—you may wonder how a dolphin manages to fit so much in. The truth is: yes, sometimes dolphins may exaggerate a little. But if a little embellishment is good for entertainment—to pass the time at the concert until the act arrives onstage—it's a lie for a good cause. The end justifies the means.

The best stories of all happen on vacation. While whales prepare dips in their camper vans at the lake and sharks enjoy the view from their private infinity pools, dolphins head off to all-inclusive beach resorts. Predictably, the backpack is packed on the morning of departure: flip-flops, swimming gear, two t-shirts, and a box of beer.

And all things considered, the vacation is a good one. By the time the bus turns onto the driveway, it's shaking with a rousing chorus of "Sweet Caroline." Dolphin vacationers are not averse to a substance or two, the key among them being Red Bull. *Sleep? What for? There's time for that when I'm dead*, the dolphin thinks.

When the party dolphin returns two weeks later and is asked what they have been up to, they are blank. "I don't know," they say, "but I know it was incredible." And the other animals in this scenario? As dolphins disembark the bus, they thank the whale driver, and back at the office, the shark is counting the profits.

Just as for whales and sharks, there are special dolphin-friendly TV shows with shiny ad spots that compete for attention during the commercial breaks. Any celebrity reality TV show is a dolphin favorite, as is any kind of show with outrageous stunts and pranks.

Of course, dolphins alone do not a TV show make. While they are (narrowly avoiding) breaking their necks, the whale is patiently standing by in a Red Cross t-shirt. The shark is the glittering sponsor, busying themselves by hanging advertising banners before the event kicks off. Once you start to think about it, it's not hard to see where each types fit in.

The dolphin is a born survivor: one who is guaranteed to find a solution to any tricky situation. Sometimes it might not fit the problem, but the dolphin always tries its best. And if it fails, at least it has enough confetti to brighten up the scene.

Dolphins can be extravagant when it comes to their looks. Dolphin women are often adorned with so much makeup that they can send a passing chameleon into cardiac arrest. And where did the chameleon come from? "Well, you'll never believe that one," grins the dolphin woman, launching into her next tale.

Which of your friends and acquaintances prefer to solve problems by throwing glitter at them? Take a moment to write down their names.

The Owl

"Why a flying animal, not a swimming one?" Ladies and gentlemen: I don't need a crystal ball to know that many of you will be asking this. In fact, this is just the type of question that an owl might ask. The owl defies the previous pattern, and an owl type will feel compelled to investigate this immediately.

Owls need patterns, and we need owls—to understand why confetti falls when we throw it up, and because, of course, not *every* problem can be solved by sprinkling confetti on it.

In many cases, the only "confetti" in an owl's life will be the scraps of paper in its nesting hole. These are not thrown in the air but sensibly disposed of in the recycling bin on a quiet day. The owl likely knows exactly how many pieces they need ("Two per sheet at 130 sheets a week, and fifty-two fewer in weeks with a holiday.") The owl has it all worked out. The dolphin, meanwhile, was engaged elsewhere as soon as the word confetti was mentioned—they prefer the colorful stuff, anyway.

By now, you might have noticed that dolphins and owls are different types of people. While the dolphin is busy building castles in the sky, the owl is checking the static calculations. Once it has done so, it issues a conclusion: air is unsuitable as a building material, and confetti will endanger the rainforest.

Owls are pragmatists, problem-solvers, and thinkers. If it isn't already a reality, the owl will make it so (and for that, we thank them). Owls in nature have 360-degree vision, good eyes, and incredible patience. Their human counterparts are similar. First, they weigh up all the possible outcomes; then, they mull things over in peace.

To describe owls in terms of a single archetypal question is impossible because owls ask questions all day long. One might even imagine that this is how Swiss cheese was created—that at some point, an owl was trapped in the dairy and poked holes in the Emmental with its incessant prods. Curiosity is how new things are made. In short:

> Owls are put on this planet to explain things
> to the rest of us.

For an owl, nothing is explained by "That's just how it is." Owls need to be able to check the facts. If you console a broken-hearted owl with "There are plenty of other fish in the sea," you'd better have their names, photos, and addresses in hand—filed in alphabetical order.

If you're looking for an owl at a party, you'll almost certainly find them engrossed in a serious conversation. Small talk is not for owls. Of course, this doesn't mean that you can't talk to them about the weather—it's just that afterward, you'll know why global warming is happening, and when the next ice age is coming, and how to survive it. For an owl, this is simply what weather chat looks like. Owls like to impart knowledge without being asked. They're sometimes exhausting but always informative.

If you manage to recruit an owl for your move, be sure to expect a schedule in advance with a contingency plan and a backup plan. If you're interested, the owl will gladly calculate how likely this is to be needed—and honestly, which of us isn't curious to know?

To be safe, you should cancel your previous plan, give the owl all the details, and check into a spa for the day. When you arrive at your new place in the evening, everything will have arrived in one piece, the water and internet will be connected, and the neighbors will already have a small gift. Sounds perfect, right?

Well, yes—except that, unlike the whale, the owl will likely not do this for "free." Owls need loyalty and reciprocity, which means you also have to be there for them when they need you. Since owls never forget, I recommend you follow through on the favors you owe them. If you don't, they will leave your life silently, as real owls are known to do, and you won't be able to do anything but watch.

If you need an owl in your life, I recommend you take a cultural vacation, where you'll find owls as far as the eye can see. In general, owls are highly appreciative of keen learners: those who plan trips with meticulous schedules and formidable to-do lists to check off. While a dolphin will find such a trip lacking in spontaneity, a predominantly owl type will embrace this as a chance to relax. Providers of such vacations know their customers well. They know that owls love painstaking planning and that the best thing they can do is to take care of it for them.

This makes owls happy, though it cannot preclude that they may recalculate the route (it may have been a dolphin in the office doing the planning, after all). Trust is good, but control is better: another guiding principle of our owl friends.

Owls like to stay close to home. If they have a free weekend, you'll find them packing their car to the brim and heading off for a weekend in the country. The car, of course, is packed the night before—and the packing plan was created in Excel two months beforehand, an optimized version of the one from previous year.

As you might expect, the owl packs for every eventuality. If a nuclear attack and an outbreak of measles hit the countryside, the owl could survive with no problems at all—especially as part of a whale-owl partnership. Whales and owls are a dream team. Armageddon could hit, and they could save the whole of humanity with the contents of their car.

If, however, the owl is married to a dolphin (out of love, or for other inexplicable reasons), and if the owl leaves the dolphin to pack using the plan, the result will be similar to the flat-pack furniture. Nothing is checked off, though the car is somehow full. *Fine*, thinks the dolphin. *If we're missing anything, we can buy it when we get there—never mind if it's a bit more expensive in the resort.* Needless to say, the owl is close to a breakdown, and any chance of harmony is out the window. Let the family vacation begin!

Advance airport check-in was invented for owls, who drive there twice beforehand just to make sure they know they'll make it. The main thing is that the luggage is safely loaded. Dolphins turn up late or not at all, whales arrive on time, and sharks show up thirty minutes before departure—"I have a gold card, let me through."

Want to advertise to an owl? Hobby magazines and documentaries are the name of the game. Owls love documentaries. While sharks like to flip through *Condé Nast Traveler*, owls receive *National Geographic* in the mail.

Of course, as an owl marketing manager for a large outdoor supply store, you already know this—that's why you train your employees regularly in personalized customer care. Owls know *everything* about the products they're thinking of buying because they've combed through all the relevant studies in the weeks before. Perhaps they've prepared a small presentation from which the seller can learn something—I wouldn't rule it out.

Speaking of outdoor shops: there are certain clothes you'll only be found in if you are a bona fide owl. Have you ever owned a pair of trousers that zip off at the knee? Not the most stylish, sure, but so comfy and *so* practical. And while practical also has its limits, never fear—owls are well-versed in what they are.

Owls like to think before, after, and in between. They ask questions they're planning to answer in the next breath and are rarely satisfied with the status quo. Do you recognize anyone from this description? Who are the owls in your life?

- _____
- _____
- _____
- _____
- _____
- _____
- _____
- _____
- _____
- _____
- _____
- _____
- _____
- _____
- _____
- _____

Dealing with Whales

"Giving is the new having."

Pluses: Whales are reserved, relaxed, patient, steady, satisfied, balancing, calm, interested in sharing, and empathetic.

Minuses: Whales are melancholic, phlegmatic, conflict-avoidant, and absent-minded.

The Whale in a Professional Environment

At work, a whale is a mediator, harmony-seeker, and team player who is loyal, persistent, and exhibits the qualities of a leader.

As a colleague, the whale is an absolute asset, and not just because they provide homemade cakes and make the shark a coffee first thing in the morning. Rather, the whale knows intuitively that the coffee is essential to all our survival.

Thanks to its strong sense of empathy, the whale is a valuable team player. Though whales may have weaknesses in terms of conflict avoidance, they have an unparalleled instinct for which colleagues need space, which colleagues need a stage, which ones need appreciation, which need honest praise to spur them on, and which prefer to pull the strings in the background.

Never make the mistake of believing that whales are only effective in social professions or at the secretary's desk. The whale may not be a born leader, but with the right guidance and good coaching, they can become a valuable boardroom employee. They have finely tuned antennae for the needs of colleagues and an incredible ability to discern why a team is unproductive and how that can be changed. For all the frugality that is attributed to the whale, their positive qualities should not be underestimated (and neither, of course, should their cake).

Whales are always happy to be praised for their achievements, but they are even happier to receive a person's time and attention. Whales are often left to fend for themselves, so ask how they are over a cup of coffee. Flustered at first, they will try to direct the conversation to the weather, but now that you understand this, you can simply ask again.

You might also take the time to give the whale a carefully selected bouquet of flowers or a carefully handwritten note. At first, they will dismiss such gestures and mutter an embarrassed "thanks," giving you the impression that they do not appreciate them. In truth, the whale is often far too modest in their self-perception to accept a kind act or compliment. In secret, their whale heart will be exploding with joy.

The Whale in Its Personal Life

Friend
Whales have lots of friends. They are caring, good listeners that like company.

Partner
As partners, whales are conflict-shy, easy to deal with, and like to give (sometimes too much).

Child
As children, whales are shy, reserved, daydreamers that like to share—and make great siblings!

Parent
As parents, whales are patient, caring, and attentive to all activities (they may even be on the parents' advisory board).

Whale types feel most comfortable in the community and usually have a large circle of friends. They are the ones who organize game nights, dish parties, and mulled wine at the Christmas market via WhatsApp threads with fifty-five members. A whale's greatest fear is to exclude or forget someone.

Whales do not like to dance out of line. They are reluctant to take center stage, and as such, they are great listeners. A whale friend will not only listen to your problems but help you look for a solution. From now on, it's no longer just your problem—it's both of your problems.

Whales are unobtrusive, adaptable people. They readily put their interests aside to keep the peace and make others happy.

Even as a vegetarian, a whale partner will happily go to a steak house, knowing not only that meat is the only thing on the menu but that some of it is so rare, it's practically still alive. The whale knows everything. In truth, as a passionate animal rights activist, the whale finds the steakhouse a little uncomfortable. They knows they won't find fried tofu on the menu, and of course, they would have preferred the new vegan place on the corner. But it's a special occasion, and that's enough for the whale to see their partner's eyes shining when the beef fillet, perfectly medium-rare, is set down on the table. The whale will pretend they were not hungry anyway and nibble enthusiastically on the salad garnish.

Every family needs a whale. Look around at home. If you don't find one, adopt one immediately; there is no alternative. If need be, take a family trip to a national park; here, whales are plentiful, and many will be willing to be taken under your wing.

Allow me to explain why the whale is indispensable. Whales, especially within the family, are conflict-averse and thus serve as a vital balancing force. By some ingenious power, they manage to orchestrate three days of Christmas with grumpy relatives without major damage to life, limbs, family peace, or the expensive gold-rimmed crockery. In some families, this borders on a miracle.

Christmas is a great opportunity to dig into the animal traits in your family. Among the other benefits of such reflection, you'll be sure to get everyone's gifts just right.

Perhaps you enjoy knitting scarves by the fireplace but are not sure if everyone will be thrilled to receive one. Well, of course they will. Who wants to freeze? But this doesn't mean there isn't room for a little fine-tuning.

While the whale will adore receiving any homemade gift, the shark will be more indifferent—unless, of course, it was personally crafted by Karl Lagerfeld. For the shark, you need high-quality cashmere wool and attractive wrapping—style is just as important as substance.

For the owl, choose extra-breathable llama wool from the Nepalese highlands. The key here is not to buy from the local craft store and simply make up the story. It has to be just right and should ideally be documented with an official certificate of origin. Just put the link in the Christmas card—the owl will Google it anyway.

By contrast, for the dolphin, the origin couldn't be less important. You've already thought of this, of course, and bought a brightly colored glittery variety. The finished scarf is adorned with a snowman—complete with a bright button that plays "Last Christmas"—and lo and behold, Christmas is saved. Well… maybe not. But at least the present-giving is sorted: four times scarf, four times happy, four times a splash of ingeniousness. Not so tricky, is it?

Whales not only afford stability to relationships and families but are also ideal mediators, well versed as they are in setting aside their own interests and taking a back seat. Their greatest strength is directly linked to their great sensitivity. Since they are excellent observers, they maintain a keen sense of family dynamics and will discreetly steer impending disputes into calmer waters. Simply put, whales do not like to swim against the tide. This disrupts their need for harmony and permanence.

However, even though whales can be thick-skinned, they run the risk of ignoring themselves and their own needs in favor of others. Though they'll rarely say it, even a whale needs some time out and must learn not only to look after others but also to take care of themselves.

This is something they must consciously learn. If a predominantly whale type suddenly has no one to take care of, they may feel that the rug has been pulled out from under them. In such cases, it is good for them to be able to care for themselves.

Whales draw problems to themselves: they are too happy to listen to the concerns of their fellow human beings and make them their own. However, too many problems can cloud the mind and cause the whale to fall into brooding. If a whale only cares for others and has never learned to be good to itself, it will eventually feel drained and begin to lack strength and energy. Since the whale is an important pillar of the family, other members will also suffer.

Sometimes, whales need to be kindly prompted to take time for themselves. What's the best way to plan the break? Well, the shark will select a luxurious location and, ideally, should pay for it, while the dolphin should be in attendance for the necessary levity and fun. The owl, of course, will expertly plan the whole thing. This is just an idea—as always, with the animal model, teamwork makes the dream work.

Checklist for Your Personal Growth as a Whale

- Don't allow yourself to be exploited.
- Take breaks; set aside some "me time."
- Find a hobby that has nothing to do with others' needs.
- Turn the lights on during sex.
- Try something new.
- Learn to say no.

You are great as you are, and you don't need to worry what others think about you. The truth is: others are predominantly worried about themselves.

Dealing with Sharks

"Tough times don't last—tough people do."

Pluses: Sharks are strong-willed, courageous, independent, confident, and determined.

Minuses: Sharks are unempathetic, bossy, dismissive of others, and domineering.

The Shark in a Professional Environment

At work, sharks are courageous. They see the bigger picture, and though they like to delegate low-level tasks, they are also workaholics that are willing to take on responsibility.

That's good news, as is the fact that shark types tend to confine themselves to specific habitats—namely, the executive floors of large and medium-sized companies. They might also be self-employed. Sharks go where there is space to accommodate them; if confined, there is a risk that they may bite. For a shark, thinking small is not just difficult, it's simply not in its DNA. Forcing it to do so would be like kidnapping it from the Atlantic and putting it in the neighbor's garden pond.

This makes no sense, the shark would think. *What should I do here? Drink cocktails with the goldfish before turning them into sushi?*

When I envision this scenario, I don't know who I pity more. If I could implore all leaders to heed one piece of advice, it's to never put your sharks in the neighbor's garden pond (so to speak). At some point, they will starve and die a miserable death, but only after everyone else has died, too.

Sharks are a business asset due to their strong gift of perception. In the sea, sharks can detect a single drop of diluted blood billions of times, thus tracking down their prey from over 100 meters. They can assess the situation at lightning speed and discern what will work and what won't.

In boardrooms, sharks have a nose for something completely different. Blood, diluted or otherwise, is not what they're interested in. Instead, the shark on two legs has a sixth sense for success. They can sniff out the chances of success immediately and instinctively track down any way to reach it. Once they've captured something, the shark bites firmly and never lets go. It belongs to them, once and for all, no arguments.

This can create the mistaken impression that sharks don't have a heart. They certainly do if we believe the experts—it might just be better concealed than most. Now, imagine you could win over a shark to your cause with all the flair, bite, and devotion they bring. How amazing would that be?

If you don't have a shark in your professional life, you should try to recruit one as soon as possible. Invest a year's salary and take a few weeks of vacation in Mauritius.

Sharks are doers that often have a dormant temper. Though they have many things, they have little to no reserve of patience. They solve problems and make decisions without weighing all eventualities. They don't have to, either, because as we know, sharks have a good nose for success. (If a shark is wrong, it often equates to a financial disaster, since sharks do not shy away from large sums.)

Sharks understand they take significant risks and bear immense responsibility. Not everyone is made for this. Such responsibility gives other animals sleepless nights, and a shark may suffer from this, too. However, the shark embraces the fear and does things anyway. Someone has to do it, and the shark finds that they are a better choice than most.

Sharks set standards—not just any old standards, but standards so high you can walk right under them in six-inch heels. "Step up or step out" is a principle invented by sharks that is implemented in virtually all areas of their lives, but nowhere does it apply more than at work. Sharks are workaholics—if *they* take a lot of work home for Christmas, why shouldn't everyone else, too? The standards sharks set for themselves are the same ones they apply to others, and those who do not reach them are not only laughed at but viciously bitten.

Dealing with sharks at work is easy. If you you're a straightforward communicator that provides the occasional compliment, you'll be moving in calm waters—you can even expect a Christmas bonus or a voucher from a luxury department store. As you open it, the shark will be humming "Last Christmas" and studying the balance sheets under the tree.

The Shark in Its Personal Life

Friend
Sharks need few friends. They are the "doers" of group activities, love gatherings with an individual touch, are happy to help people in whom they can see themselves.

Partner
Sharks are conflict-averse, domineering, and inexpressive.

Child
Guided by facts, shark children like their own company. As they tend to be leaders of a group, they dominate other children.

Parent
Shark parents have high expectations, create rigid structures to family life, and make decisions for others.

"Tolerance is the suspicion that the other person just might be right," said Kurt Tucholsky. A shark will not understand this sentence—for them, being right is the only option. If, contrary to expectations, the shark turns out to be wrong, they will find eloquent arguments to justify themselves; if the shark lacks this rhetorical skill, they will make themselves understood without eloquence. The main thing is that the shark is right, they might just not have been proven so yet—after all, how long did people spend thinking that the earth was flat?

It is by this same logic—and this assertion of relative bargaining power—that sharks often get their counterparts to agree, even if their opinions differ. Pitting yourself against a shark is like climbing Kilimanjaro untrained and in flip-flops: you'll be exhausted before you're halfway there. So before you throw yourself into shark-infested waters, always weigh the costs and benefits of your own energy reserves.

Simply, a shark's views are not up for debate. A shark makes a case for what they believe, then exits the scene. This can be a major relationship stressor that can drive friends and family to madness. The eventual response to this is often resignation—in the end, they simply let the shark go.

"You get to be right, and I get peace and quiet" is a familiar notion for every family in which a shark swims. Moreover, the shark doesn't have to be a parent: whole families can be dominated by shark children, who decide everything down to the color of the new suite. Parents with a shark child will know what I'm talking about, and anyone who smirks at this should try raising such a little devil themselves. To anyone who has done so, I tip my hat to you.

Sharks spend most of their time at work, where they play a leading role and rarely have to justify themselves. At home, things are much the same. When a shark is head of the family, they decide which car to buy, where to go on holiday, and which fir tree to buy from the Christmas market. The Fraser fir might be the most beautiful in the square, but if the shark has decided on the tree next to it, that's the one that will be bought. If at home, the tree turns out to be too big and more slanted than the tower of Pisa, the shark will find a reason to say it's perfect regardless—in this case, it fits like a dream under the sloping ceiling.

To maintain a happy relationship *and* get the tree of your dreams, you need to make the shark believe that starting again was their idea. "Yes, darling," you might say soothingly. "I agree with you that we should go back." This is not easy, but it *is* possible. In contrast, expecting an apology for the shark's misjudgment is a sadly futile endeavor. The admission and the new tree are enough (and at second glance, the first tree was more suitable as firewood, anyway.)

Generally, the shark is happy to be alone and even enjoys it. They probably couldn't even tell you why. This doesn't mean that they dislike or avoid relationships—they *do* like to be the one that sets the tone and makes decisions. Relying emotionally on a shark can quickly end in tears; sharks are independent in dealing with problems and challenges, so they expect others to be the same. For sharks, going to the doctor is a highly unwelcome activity, as it plays into their fear of having their fate dictated by others. It is not that the shark fundamentally disregards others' opinions; they simply think they have a better perspective.

Sharks set and achieve high goals, which makes them fascinating but also scary. Unconsciously, we all compare ourselves to our surroundings. If you surround yourself with sharks, you have exactly two options: either feel inadequate in the luster of their success, or feel inspired and spurred on by it. Never forget that *you* choose your reaction. We both know which decision will help you progress more!

Checklist for Your Personal Growth as a Shark:

- Don't let yourself be blinded by compliments.
- Try to become more cooperative.
- Google "empathy." If necessary, have a whale explain it to you.
- Take time off from work without feeling guilty.
- Learn to be patient—good things take time.
- Be lenient with yourself.
- Learn to apologize and to see it as a sign of strength.

You are great as you are and don't need to set ever-loftier goals to prove it. The truth is that the important people in your life do not measure your value by your success.

Dealing with Dolphins

"A little party never killed nobody!"

Pluses: Dolphins are humorous, emotional, curious, spontaneous, sociable, easy-going, and optimistic.

Minuses: Dolphins are naive, self-centered, disorganized, and prone to exaggeration.

The Dolphin in a Professional Environment

Dolphins are enthusiastic, inspiring, creative, problem-solving, and innovating.

Even in their professional life, the dolphin has limitless creativity and is prone to building the biggest castles in the sky. Their mind maps are legendary and promise nothing less than world domination. Simply, the dolphin sprinkles too little confetti at the feet of facts. But what can be exhausting for the dolphin's colleagues can be a big win for the company. Admittedly, dolphins are not at the front of the pack on planning and implementation, but they *are* far ahead in terms of concepts and innovations—and to realize the possible, you first have to dare to dream the impossible.

Dolphins are not afraid to express their ideas since they rarely worry about what others think anyway. They generally engage in little serious thought, instead preferring to fantasize and dream. A drab work environment does nothing to inspire them. Once their interest has been lost, they will slouch at their desk and draw colorful hearts until the end of the day, just like they did at school. After all, what is learnt in the cradle lasts to the grave.

Unbox Your Relationships

Even more likely is that the dolphin will quit and look for a more exciting job. Certainly, companies that are not moving forward have nothing to offer dolphins creatively—not when there are so many more interesting options. Put a paddling pool in the courtyard or a foosball table in the lounge in summer. Convert offices into colorful think tanks, with yellow sofas, ball pits, or beach volleyball in the parking lot. It's doesn't take much to help people thrive. Give the creative ones something to play with and they'll always surprise you with the results.

If innovation and change are occurring in the workplace, it's best to let a dolphin communicate it. It's no secret that change is feared—something new and unknown can be quite scary. Since fear is a visceral response, it's no use to try and rationalize your radical plans. That's about as useful as taking Smarties for a headache. Instead, let the dolphin plan the campaign and counter the fear of change with the desire for something new. Dolphins can also be afraid, but their curiosity for new things is always much greater, and they have the gift of infecting others with it, too.

How do you keep a "business dolphin" motivated? Well, if a cake with a person in the middle sounds like too much effort, how about a surprise party—even a small one, among close colleagues? While the owl would find this a colossal social undertaking, the dolphin would positively relish the occasion: such a gathering appeals to their social nature, lets them feel your appreciation, and will certainly be remembered fondly. If there's no time for a party, a dolphin might also thank you for a carefully chosen concert ticket—presented, of course, in a card hung on a helium balloon. When the dolphin opens the card, the feel-good music begins to play: "Don't worry, be happy."

The Dolphin in Its Personal Life

Friend
Dolphins are active and have many friends. They love people, do not bear grudges, and see the positive in everything.

Partner
As partners, dolphins are playful, emotional, forgiving, uncomplicated, and easy-going.

Child
Dolphin children are lively, energetic, creative, curious, and active.

Parent
Dolphin parents revert to being children. They turn the house into Disneyland, and can easily recognize themselves in their children.

Unbox Your Relationships

If you arrive at a new acquaintance's apartment and wonder whether you've somehow stumbled onto the set of *The Lion King*—because the host presents you with a paper mane and asks you to sit on a throne until he's put Simba to bed—you can probably guess what kind of animals you're dealing with. Just use the extra time to practice your warmup—"Hakuna Matata," indeed.

When a dolphin couple throws a party for their young child, the scenes are similarly vibrant. Out comes the Smarties-covered birthday cake, and the parents' faces are as excited as if they were the birthday boy or girl themselves. They enjoy the costumes and face paint a little too much. Though they hate to admit it, dolphins suffer from a heavy dose of Peter Pan syndrome—they simply don't want to grow up! In most cases, they have tried it briefly and found it pointless. Since then, an air of Disney has prevailed in the home—and who better than the children to use as an excuse?

If the children of dolphin parents inherit their dolphin traits, this can provide rare fun for all. If, on the other hand, a dolphin couple has an owl child (because, after all, the universe loves to challenge us), this will also be an interesting ride. At four years old, the little owl will patiently explain that Disneyland is fiction: "You know, life is quite serious, actually." And just in case it hasn't got through, they'll illustrate their thesis by painting a picture. Take a deep breath—they're an owl, and that's what owls do. Take them lovingly in your arms and enjoy sprinkling a few flakes of confetti here and there without them noticing. You speak owl now—you can do that.

You can recognize dolphin children by the fact they've broken every bone in their bodies by the tender age of four. But hey, that's a small price to pay for feeling like Superman: sometimes you just need to believe you can fly.

As a partner or friend of a dolphin, you'd be well advised to learn a little spontaneity. "I'd like to have my morning coffee with a view of the Eiffel Tower, please," a dolphin might decide on a Saturday evening. Two hours later, they'll be sitting on a plane—with or without you.

Outwardly, dolphins often appear somewhat superficial; in truth, they are not the most deep-thinking creatures. Brooding, deeply philosophical thoughts about the meaning and minutiae of life are not things the dolphin likes to engage with. Rather, they prefer to keep things light. If you come to the dolphin with a problem, there is a good chance they'll dismiss it with a casual, "It'll be fine." If you're lucky, you might get a bar of chocolate and a query as to whether you're feeling better. Unfortunately, for all its good qualities, the dolphin is not the best listener; it usually prefers to talk about itself.

But more than any other type of animal, the dolphin has the precious gift of seeing the positive in every situation. If you need a little lightness in your life, hum a happy tune and invite a dolphin in. If a real problem comes along—something that needs more than positive vibes, chocolate, and glitter—you'll need to make this explicitly clear. Then, the dolphin will listen. But keep it short: you never know how long their attention will last.

Unbox Your Relationships

The often-limitless naivety of the dolphin also tends to get them into trouble. It does not come naturally to dolphins to recognize the tactics or malice behind an intention, which makes it easy to deceive them or to sway them to bad choices. A dolphin seldom checks what is behind the shower of confetti; instead, they dance through it and are ultimately disappointed by empty promises.

The dolphin's rather undiscerning nature, which affords little weight to planning and thus more to spontaneity, can get it into situations that an owl would long since have exposed as a ruse. Crucially, however, a dolphin does not let a bad mood spoil the good thing for long. A dolphin is never resentful, least of all toward itself. Simply shake off the confetti—the next adventure will definitely be a happy one.

Checklist for Your Personal Growth as a Dolphin:

- Sometimes, silence is golden.
- Don't overdo it.
- Learn to persevere, even when things are not "fun."
- Read contracts before you sign them.
- Exercise sensitivity regarding your fellow human beings. Be dependable.

You are great as you are, and your stories don't always need the extra embellishment. The truth is, even without exaggeration, your life is still more exciting than everyone else's.

Dealing with Owls

"There is a problem for every solution."

Pluses: Owls are effective, organized, deep-thinking, and down to earth.

Minuses: Owls are unspontaneous, pessimistic, moody, and phlegmatic.

The Owl in a Professional Environment

In the professional arena, owls are problem-solvers, tacticians, organizers, planners, and perfectionists.

The owl needs structure and planning at work to perform at their best. Order, set break times, regular meetings, and clear agreements— these are essential for an owl to feel comfortable. Owls can be found wherever accuracy and precision are key: in research, medicine, and (perhaps unexpectedly), in art. Many artists have a high percentage of owl in their personality profiles. If you think about it, aesthetics is nothing more than precisely coordinated visual harmony. Nuance plays a pivotal rule.

It is not surprising that excellent doctors have a high percentage of owl in their personality profiles as well. In an ideal world, I'd have the surgeon take a personality test before an operation—if the results came back as 100 percent owl, they'd be welcome to cut and stitch away. Owls are perfect matches for offices, hospitals, and laboratories—wherever order is required.

At the same time each morning, flocks of hard-working owls head to offices and accounting departments. Owls love to explain the world to others, to act as a sort of unofficial arbiter. Woe betides the dolphin who tries to turn around at the traffic light—that doesn't comply with the rules, and the owl simply must let the dolphin know.

In a team, owls are happiest organizing, planning, and writing to-do lists. List-making is an owl's favorite activity. If you make an appointment with an owl, it will note the date immediately in its (bulging) planner. While an owl can tell you in seconds what it plans to do next year, the dolphin has already misplaced the note with the time of tomorrow's meeting (or was it next week?).

Dolphins and owls complement each other perfectly in the world of work, albeit sometimes with a little friction in the gears. The dolphin likes to dream impossible things; the owl to find ways to realize them (and, of course, to note in the margin that the idea has never been done before). *The first time must come some time*, the owl thinks, *and why not now?* The owl is not afraid of challenges, neither of the occasional inevitable failure. If a door closes, the owl simply opens it again. That's how doors work (and someone invented this once, too).

Left alone, however, owls and dolphins have the potential to drive each other mad. A mediator is essential, and a whale would be more than happy to step up the plate. With their high emotional intelligence, whales can deal with both types of people skillfully and blow confetti from the engine as needed.

Without the whale's moderating influence, the dolphin is an unchecked force. Its castles in the sky are sketched in sprawling, colorful mind maps—with music and a bubble machine to bring the presentation home, of course. The poor owl swivels on its chair, eyes wide and getting wider. It chews concernedly on a pencil, waiting patiently for a PowerPoint with any semblance of orienting structure.

Have you ever witnessed a person's eyes get wider and wider over a conversation? These were most probably the eyes of an owl. "I'm still thinking about the problem," they want to tell you, "but I lost my train of thought an hour ago and have been trying to find it ever since."

Do you have any owls on your team? Give them checklists, facts to hold onto, highlighters, and sticky notes to jot down their thoughts. If you want projects to get done, you need owls in your corner—and you must work for it. If personal relationships don't fall from the sky, why should business ones?

What do you give a business owl for its birthday? Please, no flowers; flowers are for whales. Books are always welcome—or if you know the owl slightly better, a travel guide or a coupon for the outdoor shop. Relationships depend on us depositing into our shared accounts. If you take the trouble to think about it, you'll get the currency right on the first try.

The Owl in Its Personal Life

Friend
As friends, owls are good listeners. They are reliable, sensitive, and idealistic.

Partner
Owl partners are empathetic, loyal, reliable, supportive, and deep-thinking.

Child
Owl children are reserved, resourceful, creative, and like their own company.

Parent
As parents, owls have high expectations. They are firm and love order.

Owls do not merely seek to explain life with facts; they are also the deepest thinkers of the four types and engage earnestly with topics that command their attention. Owls hand-pick the people in their lives and do not feel comfortable in large groups—they prefer to meet one-on-one for a glass of wine and spend hours philosophizing, both about the grape variety and the meaning of life. By the end of the evening, you'll likely know it, too.

Owls have an inherent skill for recognizing the motives of their fellow human beings and analyzing problems. This makes them deep companions—ones who can, however, quickly drive friends and romantic partners crazy with their seriousness. You'll often wonder at the minutiae that can be questioned and philosophized in an endless loop. Credit to the Emmental from the earlier chapter—it really did its best to withstand the pecks.

For an owl, decisions affecting family life are large-scale projects in which nothing can be decided "on the fly," "spontaneously," or "by gut feeling." There could be many, many empirical values to consider.

Review sites were invented for owls. In fact, they might be the only animal that continues researching after a purchase and gets annoyed months later about their "hasty decision." As a partner, you must learn to endure that.

When choosing a partner, the owl is as meticulous as if it were researching a solution for world peace in the lab. They examine closely, weigh up, write lists of pros and cons, compare, and often remain single due to indecision. A small side note for my owl friends: the selection rarely becomes of higher quality over the years.

If you're looking for an owl as a partner, head straight to Elite Singles. After all, what would an owl do with Tinder? They cannot possibly make decisions on pictures alone. And while an owl takes a while to decide, once they have done so, their relationships are stable. The owl has a hard time making changes. Breakups pull the ground from under their feet, and they sometimes forgets that they can fly.

Checklist for Your Personal Growth as an Owl:

- Do something crazy: buy colorful confetti!
- Accept that life is not always predictable.
- Don't be afraid of change.
- Learn to forgive.
- Don't hesitate so much—just do it!
- Stop doubting everything, including yourself.
- Learn to trust.
- Be patient with people who don't think so deeply.

You are great as you are, and you don't always have to fact-check yourself. Once you begin to trust in yourself and your skills, life will become a magical journey.

Childhood through the Animal Lens

"The way we talk to our children becomes their inner voice."

—PEGGY O'MARA

Researchers disagree about how exactly our personal animal mix is formed—how much is predetermined in the womb, and which parts we acquire over the course of our lives. What's much clearer is that it doesn't take long to identify someone's predominant type: it's often evident within the first few years of a child's life. These first years are heavily influenced by whether parents recognize and speak their child's animal language, which is why I encourage parents to try to do so. If a parent has a different profile than their child, particular challenges can arise. In this case, the parent must have patience—with themselves as much as with their little one.

I love taking my children Maya and Emil to kindergarten. When the children arrive in the morning and hang up their coats, I almost have the urge to take out my popcorn—though as a dolphin, naturally, I forget it every time. Once you've finished reading this book, I promise that you, too, will find a whole new fascination in morning drop-off. These little humans are infinitely intriguing to me in their variety. Picture the scene:

Paul takes off his coat before he's even stopped walking and flings it, Batman-style, in the direction of the coat hook. The hook is inevitably missed, and the crumpled, inside-out anorak falls to the floor. Little Annie, who's standing next to him, turns it the right way out, straightens it, and hangs it on the right hook before even stopping to take off her own. As she does so, she's jostled by Lucas, who insists on hanging his coat on the hippopotamus hook. It's not his, and he's been told so a million times, but it doesn't make a lot of difference; he likes the hippopotamus hook more, and that's where he hangs his things. Nellie, who's watched the whole thing, groans, hangs Lucas's coat on the right hanger, sorts the shoes into a row, and takes Annie's hand. Like most mornings, this boisterous performance has caused a little anxiety to flash across her face.

I nibble on my virtual popcorn and bid my daughters goodbye for the day, wishing them a magical, adventurous day with a tight hug—their own animal language.

Can you imagine which animal types Annie, Paul, Lucas and Nellie are?

If you have children, godchildren, nieces, or nephews: which animal types do you see in them? Are they dolphins, owls, whales, sharks, or some combination?

- _____
- _____
- _____
- _____
- _____
- _____
- _____
- _____
- _____
- _____
- _____
- _____
- _____
- _____
- _____
- _____

Unbox Your Relationships

Love through the Animal Lens

By now, it should be clear that our world, with all its different animals, is a highly colorful and exciting place. We need the variety of species and the character traits they bring—otherwise, things would quickly get boring. But what about when it comes to relationships? In matters of love, some animal pairings are ideal, and others are disastrous.

We all know the saying "opposites attract"—and it contains more than a hint of truth. Opposites are exciting. Opposites give us access to things we don't have, to the unknown, perhaps even to the things that make us complete. If two people are the same, things can rapidly get stale. Eventually, the only change of temperature in the bedroom is the draught in the morning when the windows are opened.

What does attraction look like when we deal with the "other," the unknown? Well, psychologists say that when opposites are *too* stark, they can only sustain an attraction for a short time: a flirty conversation, a thrilling affair, or a sizzling one-night stand. If you want to find your "partner in crime," it's important that you have at least some similarities. And there are many potential variants for what this can look like.

You might, for example, have shared values and shared goals. Couples have a greater chance of being happy with one another if their respective parents raised them with similar value systems in place. Applied to the animal model, this means you need at least one common animal in your personality profiles, as this will always give you a point of agreement to fall back on.

It might sound a little unromantic, but on my second date with my now-wife, I placed a personality test under her nose. When I looked at the result, I knew I had to keep her. We contained almost identical quantities of dolphin and would always have that as a point of connection, even though her whale and my shark sometimes get in the way.

What, then, are the ideal animal pairs? The ones who can marry, have children, and will still (in all likelihood) be snuggling on the loveseat at ninety years old?

The Dream Teams

Owl–Whale

This pair is content to sit together and philosophize about life. More precisely: the owl philosophizes, and the whale is happy to listen, sometimes in a campervan in the Swiss mountains, sometimes in a battered old station wagon by the beach. They tackle the predictable pitfalls of life with the pleasure of homemade comfort dishes—a great fit!

Dolphin–Shark

A pair made for each other that loves nothing more than to talk about themselves. One goes skiing in Saint Moritz, the other attends the indoor ski run in the next city—but there is just enough compromise to make it work. When the occasion is right, the shark is happy to raise a glass on the indoor slopes, and the dolphin to celebrate at the luxury chateau. Perfect!

Animals That Can Work Together, but Might Require a Little Couples' Therapy

Shark–Owl

The shark books the couple's summer holiday in Bali before the owl's had a chance to read the hotel reviews, which can cause some conversational sparks to fly. On the positive side, however, the owl's unrelenting, intellectual nature empowers them to stand up to the shark, which both sides can embrace as a source of enrichment. Not bad!

Dolphin–Whale

As the dolphin indulges in the party lifestyle, the whale is busy making sure their partner is cared for. This can quickly result in a disparity. But if the whale can learn to see the dolphin's nonchalance as a healthy counterbalance to their pensiveness, and if the dolphin can learn to see the whale's caring as a valuable resource, the two can have a future. It's workable!

Which Combinations Should Be Avoided at All Costs?

Dolphin—Owl

The dolphin, too lackadaisical; the owl, too thorough. Even the first date is likely to be a challenge, and in most cases, nothing will come of it. Picture the scene: the dolphin wants to go skydiving while the owl is trying to calculate how many people have met a sticky end in the last twenty-four hours alone. It doesn't take long for things to get difficult.

Whale—Shark

The whale, too caring; the shark, too brash and energetic. There's not much more that can be said about these two. While the whale does everything for the shark and loses itself completely in the process, the shark quickly gets bored and looks for someone who'll stand up to them. An almost impossible combination.

When a pair are both the same type, it's important that at least partial aspects of their personalities are different. Always remember the draught in the bedroom!

Have you discovered your parents' animal combination, or perhaps that of your own relationship?

- _____
- _____
- _____
- _____
- _____
- _____
- _____
- _____
- _____
- _____
- _____
- _____
- _____
- _____
- _____
- _____

Which Animal Are You?

Discover the Animal(s) Hidden Inside!

Go online and do the test at:
https://tobias-beck.com/en/personalitytest

My Results			
Now, take your test results and transfer it onto the scale below:			

| Whale | Shark | Dolphin | Owl |

Share your results with your loved ones. Once you are aware of your animal mix, and that of the people in your life, you can #unboxyourrelationship.

The End

A Story by Chris Rogers

A long, long time ago, there was an island that was home to all human emotions: high spirits, sadness, clearness of conscience, and all the other emotions that humans can feel. One day, the emotions were told that the island was going to sink, so they prepared their ships and left. Only Love wanted to wait until the last possible moment.

Right before the island sank, Love asked for help. Vanity was passing by on a luxurious ship. "Vanity," she asked, "can you take me with you?"

"No, I can't. I have a lot of gold and silver on my ship, and I need it to be able to look at my reflection. There's no room for you."

Then, Love asked Pride, who was sailing by on another equally magnificent vessel. "Please, Pride," she said. "Can you take me with you?"

"I can't," Pride said. "Everything on here is so perfect. There's a chance you might damage it."

Love pleaded with Sadness, who also happened to be passing by. "Sadness, please take me with you!"

"Oh, Love," came the reply. "Sorry, but I'm so sad that I simply must be alone."

Suddenly, there came a voice. "Come, Love, I'll take you with me." The voice was that of an old man. So relieved and thankful was Love that she forgot to ask for the man's name.

The old man left when they arrived at land, and all the emotions gathered in a group. Love knew that she owed the man her life. She turned to Serenity. "Serenity," she said, "can you tell me who it was that helped me?"

"That was Time," said Serenity.

"Time?" said Love. "Why did Time help me?"

"Because only Time understands the importance of Love in our lives," Serenity said.

Further Reading

Bauer, Mario C., and Christian Rogers. *The Teddy Bear Is Everywhere.* Netherlands: Aperitivo International BV, 2014.

Brown, Brené. *The Power of Vulnerability.* Louisville, Colorado: Sounds True, Inc. (Audible), 2013.

Chapman, Gary. *The 5 Love Languages: The Secret to Love that Lasts.* Chicago, Illinois: Northfield Publishing, 2015.

Gottman, John, and Nan Silver. *The Seven Principles for Making a Marriage Work.* New York: Harmony Books, 2015.

Sherman, Lauren E., Ashley A. Payton, Leanna M. Hernandez, Patricia M. Greenfield, and Mirella Dapretto: "The Power of the 'Like' in Adolescence: Effects of Peer Influence on Neural and Behavioral Responses to Social Media." *Psychological Science* 27, no. 7 (May 2016): 1027-1035. https://doi.org/10.1177/0956797616645673.

Acknowledgments

The more I learn from the books I read and the seminars I attend, the clearer it becomes to me that I don't know anything at all. I am constantly confronted with worlds that are colorful and new and I've made it my life's work to explore them such that others might gain as much from them as possible.

If there's one thing that remains constant, it's my deep love for my family: my wife and best friend Rita, and my children, Emil and Maya. There's also my parents, Erika and Horst, and my siblings, Johanna, Nadine, and Olaf.

I love my friends, almost all of whom know me from a time when I was neither famous nor financially secure, and who repeatedly helped pull me back to the ground when I flew too close to the sun.

I love my team and the "Bewohnerfrei" crew: thank you for being by my side come what may, through thick and thin.

I love every minute of my life, and I always remember to practice gratitude. I know that each of us has only a limited number of heartbeats and that none of us know when our own personal countdown will begin.

A huge thank you must also go to Stephanie Brehm, who has a wonderful gift for turning words into profoundly affecting diamonds of wisdom.

Without all of you, this book wouldn't be what it is.

About the Author

Tobias Beck began his professional life as a flight attendant with learning difficulties and is now one of Europe's most in-demand speakers. As the recipient of multiple awards from Germany's prestigious *FOCUS* magazine, he has reached millions through his speaking, his online resources, and his first book, *Unbox Your Life!* (GABAL 2018), which quickly became a bestseller. His *Bewohnerfrei*® podcast, which explores ways to live a life free of energy vampires, took the number-one spot on the iTunes download charts immediately following its release. Various big-name CEOs have recruited him as a personal advisor, and his seminars are attended by hundreds of thousands of enthusiastic fans. As a school speaker, he deploys humor and cleverness to educate pupils on the principles of success and the psychology of motivation.

Learn more about Tobias Beck at: www.tobias-beck.com

Mango Publishing, established in 2014, publishes an eclectic list of books by diverse authors—both new and established voices—on topics ranging from business, personal growth, women's empowerment, LGBTQ studies, health, and spirituality to history, popular culture, time management, decluttering, lifestyle, mental wellness, aging, and sustainable living. We were recently named 2019 *and* 2020's #1 fastest-growing independent publisher by *Publishers Weekly*. Our success is driven by our main goal, which is to publish high-quality books that will entertain readers as well as make a positive difference in their lives.

Our readers are our most important resource; we value your input, suggestions, and ideas. We'd love to hear from you—after all, we are publishing books for you!

Please stay in touch with us and follow us at:
Facebook: Mango Publishing
Twitter: @MangoPublishing
Instagram: @MangoPublishing
LinkedIn: Mango Publishing
Pinterest: Mango Publishing
Newsletter: mangopublishinggroup.com/newsletter

Join us on Mango's journey to reinvent publishing, one book at a time.

CPSIA information can be obtained
at www.ICGtesting.com
Printed in the USA
LVHW031212081021
699916LV00004B/4